Spirituality of Later Life: On Humor and Despair

Spirituality of Later Life: On Humor and Despair has been co-published simultaneously as *Journal of Religious Gerontology,* Volume 16, Numbers 3/4 2004.

Spirituality of Later Life: On Humor and Despair

Rev. Elizabeth MacKinlay, PhD, RN
Editor

Spirituality of Later Life: On Humor and Despair has been co-published simultaneously as *Journal of Religious Gerontology*, Volume 16, Numbers 3/4 2004.

Routledge
Taylor & Francis Group
LONDON AND NEW YORK

First published 2004 by The Haworth Press, Inc
10 Alice Street, Binghamton, NY 13904-1580

This edition published in 2012 by Routledge
2 Park Square, Milton Park, Abingdon, Oxon OX14 4RN
711 Third Avenue, New York, NY 10017, USA

Routledge is an imprint of the Taylor & Francis Group, an informa business

Spirituality of Later Life: On Humor and Despair has been co-published simultaneously as *Journal of Religious Gerontology*, Volume 16, Numbers 3/4 2004.

The development, preparation, and publication of this work has been undertaken with great care. However, the publisher, employees, editors, and agents of The Haworth Press and all imprints of The Haworth Press, Inc., including The Haworth Medical Press® and The Pharmaceutical Products Press®, are not responsible for any errors contained herein or for consequences that may ensue from use of materials or information contained in this work. Opinions expressed by the author(s) are not necessarily those of The Haworth Press, Inc.

Cover design by Kerry E. Mack

Library of Congress Cataloging-in-Publication Data

Spirituality of later life: On humor and despair / Rev. Elizabeth MacKinlay, editor.
        p. cm.
    Includes bibliographical references and index.
    ISBN 0-7890-2731-3 (alk. paper)-ISBN 0-7890-2732-1 (pbk : alk. paper)
    1. Older people-Religious life-Congresses 2. Older people-Pastoral counseling of-Congresses 3. Wit and humor-Religious aspects-Congresses 4. Despair-Religious aspects- Congresses I. MacKinlay, Elizabeth, 1940-
BL625.4.S65 2005
259′.3-dc22   2004018867

ISBN - 978 0 7890 2732 0

Spirituality of Later Life:
On Humor and Despair

CONTENTS

ABOUT THE EDITOR

Rev. Elizabeth MacKinlay, PhD, RN, is both a registered nurse and a priest in the Anglican Church. Rev. MacKinlay is Director of the Centre for Ageing and Pastoral Studies at St. Mark's Canberra. She is Associate Professor, School of Theology, Charles Sturt University and Adjunct Professional Associate-Gerontology and Spirituality in Nursing at University of Canberra. Rev. MacKinlay is Chair of the ACT Ministerial Advisory Council on Ageing.

An active researcher and writer, Rev. MacKinlay has presented many papers and workshops, including keynote addresses both nationally and internationally. She is also a visiting lecturer at the Center for Aging, Religion, and Spirituality in St. Paul, MN, USA and a member of their Advisory Board.

Foreword

Dr. MacKinlay and her colleagues have put together an excellent volume on humor. This group of articles started out as a conference and then grew into the current collection. One brief note to those who are reading this in the United States: most of the authors in this volume are Australian. Thus, words like humour are spelled correctly. In this case, the humor is in "u"!

This excellent group of articles offers some important ways of understanding the tension between humour and despair. Too often encountered when working with older adults, this tension is very real for caregivers and seniors alike. This text offers both the identification of the issues as well as many important insights into ways of employing humour into the every day work of caregiving.

James W. Ellor, PhD

[Haworth co-indexing entry note]: "Foreword." Ellor, James W. Co-published simultaneously in *Journal of Religious Gerontology* (The Haworth Pastoral Press, an imprint of The Haworth Press, Inc.) Vol. 16, No. 3/4, 2004, p. xxv; and: *Spirituality of Later Life: On Humor and Despair* (ed: Rev. Elizabeth MacKinlay) The Haworth Pastoral Press, an imprint of The Haworth Press, Inc., 2004, p. xv. Single or multiple copies of this article are available for a fee from The Haworth Document Delivery Service [1-800-HAWORTH, 9:00 a.m. - 5:00 p.m. (EST). E-mail address: docdelivery@haworthpress.com].

Preface

Why a conference on humour and despair? Research in ageing and spirituality using a qualitative approach (MacKinlay 1998, 2001) had shown use of humour by older people. While it was not the purpose of that research to study humour in later life, it seemed appropriate to study the instances of humour found in the in-depth interviews, and to examine how humour was being used by these older adults. Together with Dr. Heather Thomson's work in humour and theology, this provided the impetus to consider a conference on the theme of humour and despair in later life, focusing on the spiritual process and tasks of ageing.

Against the push of the positive ageing movement, it is acknowledged that the process of ageing is not always positive. Ageing is not only about positive ageing and-in a sense-denying the ageing process, but also about decline and struggle living with an ageing body. However, it is also about transcendence of these disabilities and the joy and peace that transcendence can bring, sometimes in the face of major losses and disabilities. Part of this process is brought about through the use of humour. Many older people learn to laugh at the decrepitude of ageing. Is this a natural process? How can humour assist the ageing person to transcend their disabilities? Can humour be used therapeutically in later life?

The papers collected here attempt to address some of the challenges of the ageing process; the tasks and process of spiritual development, of hope, despair and humour. Most of the chapters were originally presented as papers at the conference: "The Spiritual Tasks of Ageing: Humour and Despair in Later Life," in Canberra, Australia, April 2003.

[Haworth co-indexing entry note]: "Preface." MacKinlay, Elizabeth. Co-published simultaneously in *Journal of Religious Gerontology* (The Haworth Pastoral Press, an imprint of The Haworth Press, Inc.) Vol. 16, No. 3/4, 2004, pp. xxvii-xxix; and: *Spirituality of Later Life: On Humor and Despair* (ed: Rev. Elizabeth MacKinlay) The Haworth Pastoral Press, an imprint of The Haworth Press, Inc., 2004, pp. xvii-xix. Single or multiple copies of this article are available for a fee from The Haworth Document Delivery Service [1-800-HAWORTH, 9:00 a.m. - 5:00 p.m. (EST). E-mail address: docdelivery@haworthpress.com].

xvii

It may be supposed that positive ageing may be a goal for those older people who do not have Alzheimer's disease. Does this mean that those with dementia cannot expect anything but despair in their remaining life? It is suggested here that life may still be worth living for those who live with cognitive decline. How do we know what the experience of ageing is for these people? The article by John Killick addresses issues of quality of life and insight of those who experience dementia, providing an excellent view of the latest thinking in dementia care. A key question asked about dementia is whether it destroys identity. While a weighty body of opinion and attitude speaks against the preservation of selfhood in the condition, in recent years, the contrary view has increasingly been put. Killick challenges the reader with the view that the capacity to embrace change in those surrounding the person is crucial to the maintenance of well-being for people with dementia.

Recently a woman suggested to me that life must indeed be much harder for older people, because they will find it harder to cope with loss and disability than younger people would. On the contrary, the process of ageing, when life is lived to the full, may result in an enhanced ability to deal effectively with losses and disabilities in later life. This is dependent on the ability of the individual to engage with the losses and disabilities and to transcend these. It is often a struggle, and the movement towards transcendence may be fraught with difficulties, with tears and laughter, with times of despair, times of hope, of joy and times of renewed spiritual growth. Words like self-forgetting (Frankl) and sanctification (Tillich) come to mind.

This book begins by setting out the major issues that challenge people in later life, things that may be involved in the move towards either integrity or despair. This is the starting point, and here it is acknowledged that Erikson's work is an essential basis to understanding this journey. It is also pointed out that this journey into ageing is not only physical and psychosocial but a deeply spiritual journey as well. It is here that transcendence comes into its own; it would seem that transcendence is worked out essentially at the depth of one's being. A living faith is central to the development of transcendence.

Later articles develop a pastoral framework of care for those who struggle with disabilities and losses in ageing, for example, the frequent experience of depression of older people, in the community and also in residential aged care. Older people who have no speech experience particular difficulties in communicating their needs and in finding meaning. Older people who are in the terminal stages of illness likewise struggle with life meaning and with questions of integrity and despair. Humour in ageing is examined in its relationship to the journey towards spiritual integrity.

What kind of pastoral interventions can be used to assist these people? Examples and case studies address these questions.

Elizabeth MacKinlay, PhD, RN

Human Despair and Comic Transcendence

Melvin A. Kimble, PhD

SUMMARY. Despair is a human emotion that robs persons of hope, vitality and meaning. This chapter introduces descriptions and insights concerning despair from literature, theology and psychology. The blending of these perspectives provides a multi-faceted descriptive picture of this human condition. The encounter with despair is challenged from a theological perspective by understandings from Martin Luther and Reinhold Niebuhr who introduce the dynamics of grace and faith. The uniquely human capacity of self-transcendence and self-detachment, especially the concepts of Viktor Frankl, are discussed as a way of releasing a person from the self-absorbing and isolating bondage of despair. Comedy provides a way of transcending and coping with despair. Humor expresses a certain heroic defiance in the face of life's most challenging experience and provides a valuable resource for the celebration of life and the divine comedy of faith, hope and love. *[Article copies available for a fee from The Haworth Document Delivery Service: 1-800-HAWORTH. E-mail address: <docdelivery@haworthpress.com> Website: <http://www.HaworthPress.com> © 2004 by The Haworth Press, Inc. All rights reserved.]*

KEYWORDS. Comedy, defiant power of the human spirit, dereflection, hope, meaning, self-detachment, transcendence

---

Melvin A. Kimble is Professor Emeritus of Pastoral Theology, Luther Seminary, and Director, Center for Aging, Religion and Spirituality, St. Paul, MN USA.

[Haworth co-indexing entry note]: "Human Despair and Comic Transcendence." Kimble, Melvin A. Co-published simultaneously in *Journal of Religious Gerontology* (The Haworth Pastoral Press, an imprint of The Haworth Press, Inc.) Vol. 16, No. 3/4, 2004, pp. 1-11; and: *Spirituality of Later Life: On Humor and Despair* (ed: Rev. Elizabeth MacKinlay) The Haworth Pastoral Press, an imprint of The Haworth Press, Inc., 2004, pp. 1-11. Single or multiple copies of this article are available for a fee from The Haworth Document Delivery Service [1-800-HAWORTH, 9:00 a.m. - 5:00 p.m. (EST). E-mail address: docdelivery@haworthpress.com].

In many quarters, despair is the global and personal mood of the times. A vintage *New Yorker* cartoon graphically depicts this: Two gurus on a mountain-side. One says to the other, "I've come here to ponder the futility of it all, but I can see that it is useless!" The reasons for this gloomy mood need not be exhaustively catalogued. They include a world where terrorist activity has become commonplace and tensions of religious and ethnic violence have erupted into large scale warfare which could culminate in a bio-chemical and even nuclear disaster, a world where homelessness and starvation co-exist with indecent affluence. In other words, a world which might be aptly described in one of Christopher Fry's plays as "a world festering with damnation" (1949, 3).

All of this filters down and festers in persons no matter what stage of their life cycle. Among those affected are the elderly who are also coping with changes and losses, crises and challenges in their more frail years. In interviews and conversations I've had with septuagenarians and octogenarians since 9/11/2001, the poignant comment that has been expressed over and over was "I have never been more depressed about the world . . . I feel a deep sense of despair about the future for my children and grandchildren."

This essay sets forth some images of despair viewed through several different lenses. These include not only psychological categories, but also can be viewed phenomenologically in a pre-scientific manner by way of the humanities, including the words of poets, dramatists and novelists. Space limitations do not allow for the inclusions of artists and musicians whose creative works also reflect despair. Despair will also be described in this essay through the lens of theologians and philosophers.

The second section of the essay will examine the various ways that the emotion of despair has been challenged and confronted. This section will include Viktor Frankl's concept of self-transcendence that introduces what he describes as "the defiant power of the human spirit" as well as his technique of dereflection. This will especially suggest the ways humor has been used as a means of confronting despair.

IMAGES OF HUMAN DESPAIR

Viktor Frankl defined despair as "suffering without meaning." For Frankl, doubting whether a person's life has meaning is "an existential despair, it is a spiritual distress rather than a mental disease" (1967, 67). It is the loss or lack of meaning to one's life that would make life worthwhile. Frankl relates the story of a physician friend who suffered from severe depression and despair after his wife died. Frankl asked him what would have happened if he had died first. "How she would have suffered," he said. I replied, "Don't you see, Doctor that great suffering has been spared her, and it is you that has spared her this suffering; but now you have to pay for it by surviving and mourning her." The friend could now see the meaning of his suffering, the meaning of his sacrifice. There was still suffering of course, but no longer despair, because despair is suffering without meaning. Frankl uses the geometric formula $D = S - M$ (Despair = Suffering - Meaning) (Frankl 1969, 118).

The state of inner emptiness of despair is characterized by an absence of hope. Cynthia Freeman, reflecting on her professional experience as a psychotherapist, describes despair "as being trapped in an egg of hopelessness. We are vulnerable to despair when we have lost our spiritual resilience, i.e., the ability to bounce back after one too many challenges" (personal correspondence to author, 2003). Doubt and despair are considered a person's worst enemy, putting us into a state of illusion that we are separated from God, our Source.

Despair is not the same as melancholy or depression. Despair, rather, has a dimension of having to do with future orientation and involves a sense of hopelessness. It attacks a person's resources which nourish and sustain one's ability to find life meaningful. One danger of despair is that you "shut down "and then retreat into isolation. Despair grows and festers in isolation. To despair is to wish one could simply not be, that one had never been born. To despair is to be vulnerable to the pain of looking into a hopeless and empty future. It is an emotional state between apathy and anguish. Sometimes it is accompanied by uncontrollable weeping and feelings of drowning in pain, of being plunged into a night of total darkness with no meaning. It is filled with terror and feelings of being adrift. The trap of despair closes off all options. The future holds no promise of relief or rescue. It is a life totally without meaning.

Viktor Frankl relates a case history of a woman artist who was struggling with her work and her relationship with God. She introduces phrases such as "lack of contact with life" and "I'm choking in a great silence. The disorder of my soul keeps growing. The moment comes when one realizes that life has no content, everything has become meaningless, one cannot find a way out of the ruins" (Frankl 1969, 166).

Graphic phenomenological images of despair can also be found in the poignant writings of poets and playwrights. T.S. Eliot, for example, in his play, *The Cocktail Party* has the main character, Edward, describing his trapped condition in life with these words:

There was a door.
And I could not open it. I could not touch the handle.
Why could I not walk out of my prison?
What is hell? Hell is oneself,
It was only yesterday the damnation took place. And now I must
live with it day by day,
hour by hour, forever and ever. (Eliot 1934, 342)

Even more poignantly, Oscar Wilde, during the time he was incarcerated in Reading Gaol, lamented: "We did not dare to breathe a prayer or give our anguish hope. Something was dead in each of us, and what was dead was Hope" (Wilde 2000, 19).

Ann Sexton describes this condition most graphically in her collection of poems, especially one entitled "The Sickness unto Death."

God went out of me
as if the sea dried up like sandpaper,
My body became a side of mutton
and despair roamed the slaughterhouse. (Sexton 1975, 40)

Theologians and philosophers have also expressed profound insights concerning despair. At the very heart of Luther's theology, for example, despair assumes a key position because it emerges so prominently in his personal struggle with God and his faith. Throughout his life, Luther was subject to acute depression. At the midpoint of his career, these episodes were so severe that he confesses, "I myself have been offended more than once, even to the abyss of despair, nay so far as even to wish that I had not been born" (Luther 1965, 59). Luther wrote to his friend, Melanchthon in 1527, "I was for more than a whole week in death and Hell, so that I was sick all over and my limbs still tremble. I almost lost Christ in the waves and blasts of despair and blasphemy against God!" (1972, 59).[1] Luther continues, "One may extinguish the temptations of the flesh; but, oh, how difficult it is to struggle against the temptations of blasphemy and despair!" (Michelet 1846, 208). This tragic rupture of relationship between creature and Creator causes an ever-defective trust, hope and joy.

Despair for Luther, and even in a more radical way for Soren Kierkegaard, involves falling into judgment about one's self and concluding that one is worthless, powerless and hopeless. This helpless, hopeless and futureless condition must be concealed from others and borne alone. God is regarded as ineffectual and unable to transform the valance of despair that negates all worth and meaning for one's life. This condition Kierkegaard describes as the "sickness unto death."

CHALLENGING AND CONFRONTING DESPAIR

How is despair to be challenged and confronted? There is obviously no self-help manual for addressing the profound condition of despair, but there are clues and insights from two disparate sources; namely, Martin Luther and Viktor Frankl. For Luther, the remedial answer is faith-but this is not an accomplishment, but rather a free gift through the grace of God. For Luther, grace can appear not only in Word and Sacrament but also in music, the company of friends, the touch of a beloved, and laughter. Each of these can be part of an in-breaking epiphany of divine compassion. Because of his own spiritual crises, Luther's suggestions have a ring of truth. Luther writes: "In this state there is nothing remaining alive but that inward groan that cannot be uttered in which the Spirit rises, moving upon the face of these waters covered with darkness . . . no one can understand these things but he who has tasted them: they do not stand in speculations . . . they lie in the inmost feelings of the soul" (Luther, 237). Luther is utterly convinced that the Spirit moves over the turbulent chaos of the human heart answering the sin of despair with the gift of new creation.

From a totally different perspective Viktor Frankl's paradigm of logotherapy includes his concept of the "defiant power of the human spirit" in overcoming distress, despair, and hopelessness. One of logotherapy's most helpful contributions to counseling and pastoral care is its stress on the "defiant power of the human spirit." While fully recognizing the unity and the wholeness of a person, the logotherapist appeals to that which is above and beyond the person's somatic and psychic nature, namely, the spirit.

The spiritual core of a person is capable of taking a stand not only toward negative and painful external circumstances and conditions, but also toward its own psychological character structure. If persons regard themselves as overworked emotional mechanisms that simply need overhauling or a helpless brain machine that has no control over and responsibility for themselves, then, tragically, they have no capacity to transcend themselves or to fashion meaning from suffering.

From a theological perspective, Reinhold Niebuhr has helpfully described this concept of the defiant power of the human spirit as follows:

Man is a child of nature, subject to its vicissitudes, compelled by its necessities, driven by its impulses, and confined within the brevity of the years which nature permits its varied organic forms, allowing them some, but not too much, latitude. The other less obvious fact is that man is a spirit who stands outside of nature, life, himself, his reason and the world. (1943, 3)

Logotherapy underscores the fact that persons are deciding beings. They exist as their own possibility! They have both actuality and potentiality. The freedom to choose and to change is ever present in a person's life, even in midst of despair. While acknowledging the limiting circumstances and conditions that are ever present in a person's life, Frankl writes:

Man is not fully conditioned and determined; he determines himself whether to give into conditions or stand up to them. In other words, man is ultimately self-determining. Man does not simply exist, but always decides what his existence will be, what he will become in the next moment. (1978, 206)

Niebuhr has written that "the essence of man is freedom."

Man is essentially 'finite freedom'; freedom not in the sense of indeterminacy but in the sense of being able to determine himself. Through decisions in the center of his being. Man, as finite freedom, is free within the contingencies of his finitude. But within these limits he is asked to make of himself what he is supposed to become, to fulfill his destiny. In every act of moral self-affirmation man contributes to the fulfillment of his destiny, to the actualization of what he potentially is. (1943, 3)

The emphasis on the concept of freedom by Frankl and by such theologians as Tillich and Niebuhr needs to be listened to by caregivers less they "bless" the life-styles of self-pitying choice-denying persons who seek them out for "counsel" and by so doing, reinforce their counselee's experience of hopelessness and meaning-lessness as they confront their present circumstances.

The awareness of possibilities and the understanding that individuals are deciding beings convey hope. Hope must be seen in relationship to freedom. To be free is to stand before possibilities. It is to transcend the present situation and see one's capacity to alter the status quo, even if limited to one's own attitude toward unavoidable suffering. Without such a concept of freedom, there could be no hope. In an age influenced by a rodentomorphic image of personhood as well as by a cybernetic ideology, the concept of freedom needs to be re-emphasized. Such persuasive statements concerning this unique capacity should be heeded by pastoral psychologists if they are to avoid the pitfall of a pan-deterministic counseling model. Frankl contends:

> Man is not 'driven,' man decides. Man is free, but we prefer to speak of responsibility instead of freedom. Responsibility implies something for which we are responsible-namely, the accomplishment of concrete personal tasks and demands the realization of that unique and individual meaning which every one of us has to fulfill. (1967, 11-12)

The technique of dereflection is introduced by Frankl to counteract the compulsive inclination to self-observation. This can be achieved only when the person's awareness is directed away from his or her disturbance and redirected toward the meaning in his or her life. The key to accomplishing this is self-transcendence. Frankl defines self-transcendence as that aspect of human existence which is "always directed to something or someone other than itself-be it a meaning to fulfill or another human being to encounter lovingly" (1984, 78).

The sense of humor is uniquely human. Specifically, humor is to be regarded as a manifestation of that peculiarly human ability which in Logotherapy is called self-detachment. Because of self-detachment, a person is capable of joking about oneself, laughing at oneself, and ridiculing one's own fears. By virtue of this capacity of self-transcendence, a person is capable of forgetting oneself, giving oneself, and reaching out for meaning to one's existence. This sense of humor and the capacity to laugh at oneself is exclusively human. As Frankl suggests ". . . after all, no computer is capable of laughing at itself, nor is a rat capable of asking itself whether its existence has a meaning" (1967, 122, 147). Frankl notes that in three Old Testament Psalms, God is referred to as "the laughing one!" (1969, 17). Some behaviorists, such as Conrad Lorenz, have pointed out that we do not take humor seriously enough. Humor may express a certain heroic defiance in the face of life's most crushing and challenging experiences. The presence of humor reveals that the human spirit has not been utterly vanquished. Where there is humor, there is still hope. Soren Kirkegaard regarded humor as the last essential stage before faith, as an incognito faith.

Norman Cousins, in his earlier work, *An Anatomy of an Illness*, and his later book, *Head First: The Biology of Hope*, theorized that humor, like religion provides a new perspective and creates a bodily condition more conducive to medical treatment. In research with cancer patients, he discovered that laughter decreases depression and despair of patients and creates a bodily condition more conducive to medical treatment (Cousins 1989, 1979).

The phenomenon of the comic is the objective correlate of humor which is the subjective capacity. The comic is experienced as incongruence from its simplest to its most sophisticated of its expressions. It conjures up a separate world different from the world of ordinary reality, operating by different rules. It is also a world in which the limitations of the human condition are miraculously overcome. The experience of the comic is, finally, a promise of redemption.

Reinhold Niebuhr, in an essay on *Humor and Faith*, sums up his view:

> The intimate relation between humor and faith is derived from the fact that both deal with the incongruities of our existence. Humor is concerned with the immediate incongruities of life and faith with the ultimate ones. Both humor and faith are expressions of the freedom of the human spirit, of its capacity to stand outside of life, and itself, and view the whole scene. But any view of the whole immediately creates the problem of how the incongruities of life are to be dealt with; for the effort to understand life, and our place in it, confronts us with inconsistencies and incongruities which do not fit into any neat picture of the whole. Laughter is our reaction to immediate incongruities and those which do not affect us essentially. Faith is the only possible response to the ultimate incongruities of existence which threaten the very meaning of our life. . . . Faith is the final triumph over incongruity, the final assertion of the meaningfulness of existence. (Niebuhr, 1946, 111-112)

Concerning the comic dimension of the human experience, Peter Berger, in his helpful analysis posits two levels of transcendence; namely, transcendence in a lower key and transcendence in a higher key that introduces the religious mode of comic experience in setting forth his explanation of this, he writes:

> The comic transcends the reality of the ordinary everyday existence. It posits, however temporarily, a different reality in which

the assumptions and rules of ordinary life are suspended. This is, as it were, transcendence in a lower key, it does not in itself have any necessary religious implications. But second, at least in certain manifestations of the comic suggest that this other reality has redeeming qualities and that are not temporary at all, but rather that point to that other world that has always been the object of the religious attitude. In ordinary parlance, one speaks of "redeeming laughter." Any joke can provoke such laughter, and it can be redeeming in the sense of making life easier to bear, at least briefly. In the perspective of religious faith, there is in this transitory experience an intuition, a signal of true redemption, that is, of a world that has been made whole and in which the miseries of the human condition have been abolished. This implies transcendence in a higher key; it is religious in the full and proper sense of the word . . . There is a secular and a religious mode of comic experience, and the passage from one to the other requires an act of faith. (Berger 1997)

Roy Eckardt clarifies this as he writes:

It needs to be noted that humor and comic dimension are incapable in themselves of any final victory over evil, suffering and the vicissitudes of life.

But such challenges are met or lived within and through some kind of faith . . . and among the byproducts of faith is a comic vision that can accept even life's incongruities under the rubric of a certain non-chalance, an accompaniment of grace . . . By virtue of the grace of God the Devil is laughed to scorn. The comic vision is fulfilled in the divine comedy. (Eckardt 1995, 123)

From her experience as a psychotherapist, Cynthia Freeman observes "The lightness of the high vibrations of spiritual humor serves to shatter the dense crystallizations of despair, thus allowing the despair to dissipate and the higher vision of the soul's lesson (always part of suffering) to come through. . . ." (Freeman personal correspondence, 5th April 2003). It is significant to note that Soren Kirkegaard observed that the more one suffers the more one has a sense for the comic (Vos 1966, 99).

CONCLUSION

The playwright, Christopher Fry, provides an appropriate summary for this essay; namely, "Comedy is an escape, not from truth, but from despair: a narrow escape into faith . . . Comedy says, in effect, that groaning as we may be, we move in the figure of a dance, and so moving, we trace the outline of the mystery" (Kirkegaard 1978, 30).

This "escape into faith" is a new understanding of the meaning of life. Fry suggests that laughter "almost amounts to revelation" (Vos 1966, 99). And the revelation of God to man is not essentially tragedy, it is rather the greatest comedy of all time: a comic action of passion, a drama of both suffering and love.

Older adults who have matured in their faith appear to have learned how to deal with despair. At difficult times in their lives they have been able to use humor not simply to cope, but to transcend. They have discovered an understanding of life that in all of its diverse conditions, including those of old age, as life lived *sub specie aeternitatis*. In doing so they have in exemplary ways demonstrated not only comic transcendence but also the defiant power of the human spirit.

NOTE

1. Letter of August 2, 1527, in *Luther's Correspondence, v.II*, ed. Smith-Jacobs, cited by Vergillius Ferm in *Cross Currents of the Personality of Martin Luther* (North Quincy, MA: The Christopher Publishing House, 1972)100.

REFERENCES

Berger, P. L. (1997). *Redeeming Laughter: The Comic Dimension of Human Experience.* New York: Walter De Gruyter.

Cousins, N. (1989). *Head First: The Biology of Hope.* New York: AP. Dutton.

Cousins, N. (1979). *An Anatomy of an Illness.* New York: WW Norton.

Eckardt, R. (1995). *How to Tell God From the Devil.* New Brunswick, New Jersey: Transaction Publishers.

Eliot, T. S. (1934). *The Cocktail Party, The Complete Programs and Plays.* New York: Harcourt, Brace and Company.

Ferm, V. (1972). Letter of August 2, 1527, in Luther's Correspondence, v.II ed Smith-Jacobs, cited in *Cross Currents of the Personality of Martin Luther.* North Quincy, MA: The Christopher Publishing House.

Frankl, V. E. (1967). *Psychotherapy and Existentialism.* New York: Washington Square Press.

Frankl, V. E. (1969). *The Will to Meaning*. New York: World Publishing.

Frankl, V. E. (1984). *The Unheard Cry for Meaning*. New York: Washington Square Press.

Freeman, F. (2003). personal correspondence to author, April 5.

Fry, C. (1949). *The Lady's Not for Burning*. New York: The Oxford University Press.

Luther, M. (1965) W.A. 18.719.8, cited by Susan Snyder in *The Left Hand of God: Despair in Medieval and Renaissance Tradition XIII*.

Luther, M. W.A. 5.385.19 *Commentary on Psalms*, in G. Rupp in *The Righteousness of God* London: Hodder and Stoughton, 1953, p. 237.

Michelet, M. (1846). *Life of Luther*. Written by himself, Collected and arranged by M. Michelet, trans. by Hazlitt. London: David Bogue.

Niebuhr, R. (1943). *The Nature and Destiny of Man*. New York: Charles Scribner and Sons.

Niebuhr, R. (1946). *Humor and Faith, In Discerning the Signs of the Times*. New York: Charles Scribner and Sons.

Sexton, A. (1975). *The Awful Rowing Toward God*. Boston: Houghton Mifflin.

Vos, N. (1966). *The Drama of Comedy: Victim and Victor*. Richmond: John Knox Press.

Wilde, O. (2000). *The Ballad of Reading Gaol. Collected Works of Oscar Wilde*. New York: Classic Books.

The Paradoxes of Humor and the Burdens of Despair

Susan H. McFadden, PhD

SUMMARY. People today often express considerable despair *about* old age and the aging process. Older adults who experience frequent losses of connections with important persons can feel considerable despair *in* old age. Nevertheless, many older people retain hope in the face of situations that elicit despair and demonstrate what gerontologists call the "paradox of well being" in later life. Often, their hope is expressed in humor. This paper traces the connections among humor, hope, and religious faith in older adults. It argues that even persons who suffer from dementia can continue to express what Viktor Frankl called the "defiant power of the human spirit" through their humor. *[Article copies available for a fee from The Haworth Document Delivery Service: 1-800-HAWORTH. E-mail address: <docdelivery@haworthpress.com> Website: <http://www. HaworthPress.com> © 2004 by The Haworth Press, Inc. All rights reserved.]*

KEYWORDS. Emotion and aging, humor and aging, despair, religious faith, paradox of well-being

---

Susan H. McFadden is Professor of Psychology, University of Wisconsin Oshkosh, 800 Algoma Boulevard, Oshkosh, WI 54901 USA (E-mail: mcfadden@uwosh.edu).

This paper was presented at a conference on "Spiritual tasks and the process of ageing: Humour and despair in later life."

[Haworth co-indexing entry note]: "The Paradoxes of Humor and the Burdens of Despair." McFadden, Susan H. Co-published simultaneously in *Journal of Religious Gerontology* (The Haworth Pastoral Press, an imprint of The Haworth Press, Inc.) Vol. 16, No. 3/4, 2004, pp. 13-27; and: *Spirituality of Later Life: On Humor and Despair* (ed: Rev. Elizabeth MacKinlay) The Haworth Pastoral Press, an imprint of The Haworth Press, Inc., 2004, pp. 13-27. Single or multiple copies of this article are available for a fee from The Haworth Document Delivery Service [1-800-HAWORTH, 9:00 a.m. - 5:00 p.m. (EST). E-mail address: docdelivery@haworthpress.com].

http://www.haworthpress.com/web/JRG
© 2004 by The Haworth Press, Inc. All rights reserved.
Digital Object Identifier: 10.1300/J078v16n03_02

When telling friends and colleagues about the invitation to present a paper in Australia on "humor and despair" in later life, I observed a curious reaction. Most simply did not seem to hear the word "despair" and immediately connected my topic to jokes about growing old. Some even started sending me copies of these jokes, which exist in abundance in cyberspace. Although this paper is most decidedly not about jokes on aging, nevertheless I was intrigued to observe the types of jokes I received, many of which seemed not to heal or transcend despair about aging, but rather to deny or even wallow in despair about aging. My experience reflects empirical studies of jokes about aging that show that the majority express negative attitudes about "physical and mental ability, appearance and attractiveness, sexual ability or interest, and age concealment" (Palmore, 1986, p. 118).

In our world today, there exists considerable despair about aging and old age. One only has to witness the burgeoning interest in "anti-aging medicine." Recently, legitimate biogerontologists forcefully responded to the false and often dangerous claims being made for various treatments and drugs that supposedly will reverse or even eliminate aging processes (Binstock, 2003). Nevertheless, the anti-aging movement continues to grow, as anyone can easily witness by entering "anti-aging medicine" into an Internet search engine. Swathed in pseudo-scientific claims to remove from human experience all vestiges of suffering wrought by the passage of time, anti-aging medicine has captured a large audience of persons seemingly in despair about growing older.

While the response to despair over aging in the form of anti-aging nostrums may be physically dangerous, other responses may be psychologically and socially dangerous. For example, some people transform despair into anger and resentment of older adults, reinforcing ageist stereotypes and legitimizing discrimination. We saw this a few years ago in the "generational equity" movement, which claimed that older people selfishly hoard resources that then are denied to young adults. Driven by what Moody (2002, p. 45) has called "apocalyptic demography," this movement exaggerated concerns over funding for the Social Security and Medicare systems in the US and fueled anger toward older people.

I witnessed a combination of anger, resentment, fear, and avoidance of older people the very first time I traveled to a gerontology conference. I arrived in California and needed to take a cab to my hotel. The friendly young cabdriver asked me the purpose of my trip and I told him about my interest in aging people. Immediately, he launched into a dissertation on his attitudes toward older people. "You want to see old people"? (I had made no such request.) "I'll show you old people. They're all standing around on the streets of a town near here. They're all short. And ugly. And they dress funny. I hate it when I have to take them any- where." I protested that surely these old people must at the very least have many good stories to tell and that perhaps he had grandparents he loved and respected. Ignoring me, he continued. "You can hardly get 'em in these Checker cabs 'cause the seats are so high. You have to get out and push them in." By now I had reached my destination, somewhat better informed about at least one young Californian's attitudes toward aging. This young man was well on his way to becoming a gullible can- didate for the elixirs of anti-aging medicine.

The despair of the young about aging, with its admixture of other negative emotions, results in large part from the inability to confer meaning on the latter part of the life span. Having first lost what Moody (1986) calls "cosmic meaning" about aging and later collective mean- ing embodied in social institutions, many people today are left only with privatized meanings that often do not stand up to the onslaught of mes- sages about the desirability of youth. This privatization of meaning has occurred in the context of a society that has failed to adapt to the chang- ing nature of aging, a situation that Matilda and Jack Riley called "struc- tural lag" (Riley & Riley, 1994). With meaning now solely resting upon the individual, it is no wonder that many persons feel despair when they anticipate later life with its inevitable losses and narcissistic insults. This despair *about* old age must be differentiated from despair *in* old age. The former has an object-old age-and in part, it is socially con- structed. The latter resides in the depths of human experience where it has existed since the first moments of life.

Human beings are born with the capacity for despair because of their inherent social nature. We see this despair on the faces of infants who receive inadequate love and attention from caregivers. First identified by psychiatrist John Bowlby (1969-1980), and experimental psycholo- gist, Harry Harlow (1959), this is the despair of a creature whose very life depends upon intimate connections to others. When these connec- tions are broken, despair quickly descends. Harlow poignantly demon- strated this when he removed rhesus monkeys from their mothers and put them in cages with wire and cloth surrogates. The infants formed what appeared to be close emotional attachments to the "cloth mothers" but in fact, they remained warped through life by their abandonment, unable to form social relationships with other monkeys in adulthood. That deep despondency revealed in the faces of babies and infant mon- keys when removed from their mothers recurs through life when inti- mate ties to others are broken. This is the despair of the widow who grieves the death of her husband and the despair of the old man who sits alone hour after hour waiting for someone to call or visit. Biologically based and psychologically devastating, this despair over severed social attachments is a hallmark of the human condition.

Older adults experience a kind of double jeopardy of despair. They live in a society that exhibits deep despair *about* old age and its apparent meaninglessness, and by virtue of their longevity, experiences of despair *in* old age recur as losses mount. Illustrating this unavoidable situation in late life, an elderly man was once asked by a friend what he did with his despair. This individual lived in a long term care center where he had few close friends. His wife suffered from severe dementia and resided in a special care unit. Having struggled with near blindness for many years, he finally underwent surgery on his eyes that instead of improving his vision, damaged it further. This situation is what led his visitor to ask him about the despair he surely must have felt. His response to the question of what he did with his despair was to "bear it" (McFadden, 1999). How did he do this? How did he manage to demonstrate what geropsychologists have called the "paradox" and "ironies" of well being (Labouvie-Vief & Medler, 2002; Ryff & Singer, 2003) by bearing the burdens of despair and at the same time, retaining hope and a measure of good cheer as amply demonstrated in the many letters he wrote to his friends? This man's life clearly illustrates what Erikson called the "paradoxes and tragic potentials of human life" (1963, p. 274). He refused to deny the burden of despair nor did he allow it to threaten his core sense of meaning in life that in his case, derived from his religious faith. His sense of ego integrity did not preclude acknowledgement of despair. Erikson intimated this when he wrote:

> Only such integrity can balance the despair of the knowledge that a limited life is coming to a conscious conclusion, only such wholeness can transcend the petty disgust of feeling finished and passed by, and the despair of facing the period of relative helplessness which marks the end as it marked the beginning. (1964, p. 134)

In the remainder of this paper, I will address the question of how people maintain a sense of integrity and wholeness while at the same time, they bear their despair. I will argue that many older adults' lives demonstrate how religious faith undergirds the "paradox of well being" by enabling them to hold onto hope while still acknowledging the contingencies of later life. And, in keeping with the theme of this conference, I will argue that authentic humor is one pathway to and expression of this faith. Humor can overcome the tension of living with paradox by fully recognizing that paradox. I am not talking about the kind of humor that denies and devalues the paradoxes of old age. That humor can neither affirm life nor lead to faith for, having split strength from weakness (or, in Erikson's terms, integrity from despair), it cannot hold in tension the ultimate paradox of life bounded by death. In order to develop this position, I will first examine humor from a psychological perspective. Next, I will relate humor to hope and will show how what I will call the "everyday humor" of older people can allow us to retain hope even when threatened by the despair wrought by the losses of dementia. This discussion will then lead to reflections on humor and faith, the ultimate source of hope for persons whose lives have leaned toward the sacred.

DEFINING AND THEORIZING ABOUT HUMOR

The task of defining humor forces the scholar to "[wade] into a brier patch of terminology" (Keith-Spiegel, 1972, p. 14). Humor resists neat definitions for a variety of reasons. For one thing, humor consists of so many different subcategories: caricature, puns, slap-stick, irony, satire, etc. Adding to the difficulty, the numerous books written on the subject frequently disagree on how to define these subcategories and some even regard humor as a subcategory of, for example, the comic. One distinction, however, on which most scholars of the subject agree, concerns the difference between humor and wit.

Freud's (1905/1960) model, which distinguished wit from humor, held that the laughter of wit (or joking) results from a savings in the energy of inhibiting the release of certain unacceptable impulses. The joke disguises these impulses and thus the individual can experience the release of laughter rather than the inhibition of impulse. Consider, for example, laughter at a joke about older men with lascivious thoughts about young women. Instead of having to disguise and inhibit dismay, disgust, or even despair about changes in sexual potency and socially defined sexual attractiveness, people laugh. For Freud, the laughter of humor represents a substitution of pleasure for a more negative emotion that might be expected in a situation. In this case, an older person might laughingly refer to creaking joints as needing oil instead of feeling self-pity over reduced mobility.

The linguistic heritage of the words "wit" and "humor" helps in understanding the differences (Gruner, 1978). The word "humor" derives from the Latin *humere* (to be moist) and the Greek *hygros* (wet) and later became associated with the four bodily fluids thought by medieval physiologists to affect temperament. "Wit" comes from the Old High German *wizzi* (knowledge) and the Old English *witan* (to know). Thus, wit is ordinarily characterized as verbal and as appealing primarily to the intellect; humor, on the other hand, need not be expressed verbally and is associated with a more wholistic, cognitive-emotional response. Or, as philosopher Marie Collins Swabey wrote, "Whereas wit is dry, tense, compressed in expression, humor tends to be loose, easy-going, meandering, often seemingly oblivious of the absurdity at its base" (1961, p. 88). This is an important distinction for the current argument being built in this paper because it focuses upon humor and not on wit (and jokes about aging).

Sometimes, older people just want to laugh and be silly. They are not seeking the keen edge of a witty joke but rather simply the liberating pleasure of laughing. When she was in her 80s, Jungian analyst Florida Scott-Maxwell (1968) described her experience of aging like this:

> I am getting fine and supple from the mistakes I've made, but I wish a notebook could laugh. Old and alone, one lives at such a high moral level. One is surrounded by eternal verities, noble austerities to scale on every side, and frightening depths of insight. It is inhuman. I long to laugh. (p. 8)

By considering reasons why Scott-Maxwell might "long to laugh," we can explore three of the most well-known theories of humor: the superiority theory, the incongruity theory, and the "relief theory." All three are pertinent to understanding the humor of older people and can be viewed not as mutually exclusive, but as interrelated.

Perhaps Scott-Maxwell longs to laugh because of the comparison she observes between her own life, and the shallow thoughts, self-indulgent behavior, and arrogant posturing of others. Her laughter then can confirm to her the meaning of the price she has paid for her "frightening depths of insight." Her longing for laughter interpreted from this point of view represents one of the oldest theories of humor and laughter: the superiority theory. With its source in the writings of Plato and Aristotle, this theory was most popularly expressed by Thomas Hobbes (1840). It claims that laughter is caused when one person feels more virtuous than another.

> The passion of laughter is nothing else but sudden glory arising from some sudden conception of some eminency in ourselves, by

comparison with the infirmity of others, or with our own formerly. (p. 46)

Hobbes was careful to note that this laughter needed to be "at absurdities and infirmities abstracted from persons" (p. 47) and not some cruel attack on a specific individual. Nevertheless, this explanation seems insufficient to explain why Scott-Maxwell longed to laugh. She expressed no opinion about her superiority over others and did not even imply that she found her younger self amusing.

Another approach would be to suppose she longed to laugh because of the incongruity she perceived between the hard-won wisdom she had attained about the "eternal verities" and the fact that death would soon nullify-for her at least-that wisdom. Or perhaps she felt an incongruity between the feelings of effervescence within and the realities of her physical condition that constrained her expression of these feelings. Finally, perhaps just having lived a long time prompted a sense of incongruity between her own, broader perspective on life and what she might have perceived as the amplification of minor concerns by younger people.

Incongruity theories, with their roots in the work of Kant, Schopenauer, and Bergson, tend to emphasize cognitive faculties because of the necessity of making a comparison between how things are, and how they are expected to be. However, neither incongruity nor superiority seems to explain Scott-Maxwell's longing. Interestingly, the answer seems to lie in Freud's essay on humor, published over 20 years after his book on wit, in which he said that humor signifies "not only the triumph of the ego but also of the pleasure principle, which is able here to assert itself against the unkindness of real circumstances" (1927/1961, pp. 162-163). This pleasure elicited by humor is, Freud said, "liberating and elevating" (p. 166).

Now, we seem to be moving closer to Scott-Maxwell's longing. While she recognized the significance of the weighty insights age and experience had brought to her consciousness, she also knew that humor and laughter might liberate her at least momentarily from them. With laughter, we feel lighter. Genuine humor-the kind Scott-Maxwell longed for-can thus be a form of transcendence, an experience possible only because she had fully recognized and grieved the contingencies of life. Indeed, she knew something about the "unkindness of real circumstances." Another way of putting this is to say that this kind of liberating humor is possible only after an individual has recognized "those unalterable realities which oppose the assertions of the narcissistic self" (Kohut, 1966, 267). In other words, the person who cannot accept suffering cannot also experience the liberation from suffering granted by genuine humor. The person capable of experiencing this kind of humor must have acknowledged suffering and the fact that suffering cannot be evaded or denied through laughter. Rather, the humor that represents, as Kohut said, a transformation of narcissism, bursts through suffering, provides a perspective on it, and momentarily relieves its pain. This kind of humor reveals a form of spiritual maturity in which an individual responds to life's limitations and inevitable suffering with trust and hope instead of bitterness and despair (McFadden, 1990).

Aging people who have transformed their narcissism, and have accepted that suffering is a part of life, may be liberated to experience humor in new ways. Unburdened by expectations constantly to be "serious" and task-oriented, they may be freed to discover "playfulness in old age" and the "liberated wonder of aged experience" (Erikson & Erikson, 1978, p. 8). This experience of playfulness and wonder may in turn make it easier to express and appreciate "everyday humor"-humor that erupts in ordinary situations. Despite all the losses and limitations that must be endured in old age, the aging person may, by virtue of discovering "leeway" for playfulness, have a greater potential for experiencing the liberation of humor than the young or middle aged adult who has not yet withdrawn narcissistic investment in images of unlimited money, power, love, or life.

Recent empirical and theoretical work on "positive psychology" has categorized humor and playfulness as important human strengths that express the virtue of transcendence (Seligman & Peterson, 2003). Other strengths that make up this virtue include appreciation of beauty, gratitude, hope, spirituality, and religiousness. Philosopher John Morreall, who has written several works about humor and laughter agrees, and states that humor supports both intellectual and moral virtues (Morreall, 1983); however, he goes even further to argue that it "is itself a virtue" (Morreall, 1999, 150). With its connection to surprise and feelings of pleasure, humor can bump us out of our mental ruts and help us think more flexibly. The idea that positive emotions open up our ways of thinking and supply personal and social resources for problem solving has received empirical support from Frederickson (2001) and others who have proposed that positivity can "broaden and build" thought-action repertoires. These positive emotions may even lead to better health, although the claims made for the effects of humor on health far exceed the empirical evidence (Martin, 2002).

HUMOR, HOPE, AND . . . DEMENTIA

Many older people are forced to fight with strength previously unknown to assert that human dignity is not the same as independence.

Sometimes, humor can help in this process by reminding others of the capacity of the human to choose to triumph over suffering. Various pathways can be taken in doing this, with humor being the one that probably elicits the most instant and positive emotions. Reflect for a moment on the older people who that young cab driver in California had to push into his cab. He treated them in an undignified, disrespectful way. Some probably spoke harshly and critically to him. Others undoubtedly accepted this treatment passively, having lost hope for any kind of better interactions with the young. Imagine, however, those persons who found a way to laugh at the situation, managing to comment critically on it and at the same time connect with the young man in a positive way. Humor, as Freud wrote, rebels, but it also bring people together in their common humanity. In situations like this, when humor affirms dignity, older people amply demonstrate what Frankl (1967) called the "defiant power of the human spirit" (p. 99). Echoing this, Hyers (1981) wrote that humor

> may express a certain heroic defiance in the face of life's most crushing defeats, an unquenchable nobility of spirit that refuses to permit a given fate or oppressor to have the last word-to be absolute. The human spirit has not been utterly vanquished. . . . Where there is humor, there is still hope. (p. 36)

Just as the young parent turns a child's fears to smiles of joy by showing how vulnerable and silly the "monsters" are, the elder gives hope to the future by accepting the losses of aging and then demonstrating with a laugh that these "monsters" cannot prevail over the human spirit. The person who has achieved the maturity of what Erikson called ego integrity can experience the liberation of humor because memories of the past have been integrated into the present without bitterness or despair; losses can be mourned without threat of ego-disintegration; and the individual can continue-despite the nearness of death-to have enough hope in a world of meaning and order to be able to generate this hope in others.

On the other hand, people with dementia have lost organized access to memories of the past. Their losses in the present are noted but then quickly forgotten cognitively, if not emotionally. Their anticipation of the future is reduced to physiological desires, in which, for example, hunger signals that a meal should be arriving soon, or sadness signals an impending visit from a loved one (even though that loved one may have died years before). Nevertheless, I would argue that by observing the everyday interactions of people living with Alzheimer's, one sees that hope is not destroyed by the disease. This is not a hope of cure, but rather the hope that arises from witnessing to that "defiant power of the human spirit" even under the circumstances of dementia. Expressions of the human spirit by persons with dementia are only possible, however, when that same spirit has not been anesthetized or even destroyed by a toxic environment (Kitwood, 1997). Such environments, where people with dementia are warehoused and treated as objects, kill hope.

Historian David Keck (1996) has called Alzheimer's Disease the "theological disease." It threatens and ultimately destroys the conscious sense of personhood that in the Abrahamic tradition is the beginning point for religious engagement with the sacred. The Psalmist may write, "I lift up my eyes to the hills-from where will my help come" (Ps. 121:1), but when the "I" has been destroyed by the accumulation of neural plaques and tangles, who searches for help? In dementia, God's grace may no longer be consciously sought, and yet because persons continue to register emotions until the very last days of the illness, grace may be conveyed through loving contact with other persons. It may even be communicated through humor.

I have written elsewhere about displays of everyday humor by people living in a dementia care unit (McFadden, Ingram, & Baldauf, 2000). The laughter and smiles accompanying their often nonsensical talk expressed pleasurable human interaction and their continuing humanity regardless of the cognitive devastation of the disease. By viewing humor in the context of hope and faith in the human spirit, no matter how "faded" (Post, 1995), we obtain a profound appreciation and respect for the power of the human spirit that breaks through even though the intellect is degraded. Mrs. G., an elderly Black woman with dementia, illustrated this well.

Mrs. G. attended a senior day center program for people with dementia. Every day, she would make the rounds of the large overheated room to sprinkle a few drops of water on all the plants. As she did so, she laughingly reminded her "friends" that "Virginia is here today my darlings to take care of you. Now let's all perk up here." Mrs. G.'s hands were grotesquely twisted with arthritis; her knees and feet were greatly swollen. She lived in an apartment with her granddaughter because she could no longer take care of herself. In spite of her physical problems and mental deterioration, Mrs. G. radiated good cheer and much humor; she exemplified the paradox and irony of well being in later life. How could Mrs. G. be so happy? In a room full of old people, many of whom spent much of the day sleeping in their chairs, Mrs. G. encouraged the plants to "perk up." And, not being satisfied with her mission to the plants, she also did her share of "perking up" her fellow center participants. To persons who fail to appreciate the radical hopefulness and faith in these acts, Mrs. G.'s comments seem crazy and meaningless. Nevertheless, even in her condition, she abundantly witnessed to the "defiant power of the human spirit." Others observing her behavior, the loving care she received from her granddaughter, the work of staff and volunteers at the day center to create the best possible environment for people with dementia might conclude that it is possible to retain hope even while dealing with very real and sometimes overwhelming challenges of dementia.

HUMOR AND FAITH

Erik Erikson (1964) observed that "hope represents the ontogenetic basis of faith" (p. 118). One observes hope and faith expressed by a widow who, just having had her cancerous colon removed, refuses to yield to the absoluteness of the diagnosis and has all her doctors and nurses laughing with her over their own sad-eye reports. There is hope and faith in the blind widower who, perceiving unhappiness in another of his frail elderly companions at a day care center, reaches back in memory to tell silly old jokes which bring a smile back to the face of the man sitting in the next chair. There is hope and faith in the husband and wife who, recognizing that their health precludes a summer vacation along their beloved coast of Maine, laughingly tell their "Meals-on-Wheels" volunteer that they will pretend the creamed tuna is Lobster Newberg while they recall for each other the joys of summers past. In all these and countless other aging people, hope and faith find expression in laughter and humor. Granted, this is not the only way of communicating hope and faith but when the humor is authentic and grounded in love and connectedness to others (rather than anger, fear, hatred, and other emotions that separate persons and create bitter, hostile humor), then both cognitively and emotionally it reveals hope and faith.

In the everyday, commonplace transactions aging people make with their worlds, the faith that undergirds their humor can be readily observed. When this faith is articulated in religious language, one can begin to discern its theological dimensions. Humor, which enables a suffering person to laugh, rests upon faith in an ultimate order that heals brokenness. This laughter is possible because of certainty of God's abiding love. Persons informed by this theological perspective recognize the limits of their humor: humor may point to what is ultimate, but itself is not ultimate. Theologian Reinhold Niebuhr (1969), who believed that "humor is, in fact a prelude to faith" (p. 134), wrote: "If laughter seeks to deal with the ultimate issues of life, it turns into a bitter humor" (p. 137). Similarly, Danish theologian Søren Kierkegaard (1944) argued that "humor is the last stage of existential inwardness before faith" (p. 259). In Christian terms, humor may affirm possibilities for overcoming brokenness and separation from other persons and from the sacred, but only a radical leap to faith can produce assurance of the grace that ultimately heals all brokenness and separation. Unfortunately, however, the Christian religion has a long history of suppressing and devaluing humor, having nurtured through the centuries what sociologist of religion Peter Berger describes as "a long line of grim theologians" (1997, p. 198).

In his book, *The Comic Vision and the Christian Faith*, Conrad Hyers (1981) traced a condescending and sometimes hostile attitude toward humor from Biblical writings through to 20th century Christian theological works. He concluded from his examination of prevalent attitudes toward humor that it was primarily viewed as:

> a light distraction from more important concerns, a playful interlude whose justification is that it may help us let off a little steam now and then or provide a cheap vacation of the mind from which we will return to work more industriously and fight unquestioningly. (p. 11)

Humor is generally held in disregard by "true believers," people who believe they are called to tasks of infinite importance. Yes, as both Hyers and Berger repeatedly caution, without the perspective of humor-the ability to laugh at the self and the self's own objects of devotion-there arises the potential for arrogance, absolutism, and idolatry. A recent study comparing fundamentalists with religious persons more open to questioning their faith found that fundamentalism predicted less "spontaneous humor creation" (p. 185) in response to descriptions of everyday life hassles, although there were no differences in terms of whether people said they used humor in coping or whether they judged themselves as having a sense of humor (Saroglou, 2002).

One could argue that there are "true believers" among those supporting the growth of "anti-aging medicine" and one might suppose that they have little ability to laugh at themselves or the various measures they take in order to stay "forever young." Their hope lies in the eradication of aging; their faith is grounded in positivism. Essentially, they have given in to despair. What they need to do is to open themselves to the witness to hope and faith evident in the lives of ordinary older adults. Many of these individuals are deeply religious. They know that ultimate hope lies in their faith in the promise of fulfillment given in their religions, whether in the covenant of God with the Jewish people, or the triumph over death on the cross, or the meaning located in submission to the will of Allah. The center of human value in all the Abrahamic faiths is not productivity, youthfulness, power, or social status, but rather the knowledge that God loves humanity. God requires nothing more than that human beings "do justice, and love kindness, and walk humbly" with God (Micah 6:8). All of these religions contain narrative traditions pointing out that along the way to religious fulfillment, the foibles and follies, the incongruities and surprises of human life and experience will be very, very funny. This is true in old age, just as it is true earlier in the life span. This kind of humor is the seal of our humanity; it gives hope and it expresses faith in meaning that triumphs over the social stereotypes that produce despair about aging and the grievous losses that plunge people into despair in old age. In this, the "defiant power of the human spirit" has the last laugh!

REFERENCES

Berger, P. L. (1997). *Redeeming laughter: The comic dimension of human experience.* New York: Walter De Gruyter.

Binstock, R. H. (2003). The war on "anti-aging medicine." *The Gerontologist, 43,* 4-14.

Bowlby, J. (1969-1980). *Attachment and loss* (Vols. 1-3). New York: Basic Books.

Erikson, E. H. (1964). *Insight and responsibility.* New York: W. W. Norton.

Erikson, E. H., & Erikson, J. (1978). Introduction: Reflections on aging. In S. F. Spicker, K. M. Woodward, & D. Van Tassel (Eds.), *Aging and the elderly: Humanistic perspectives in gerontology* (pp. 1-8). Atlantic Highlands, NJ: Humanities Press.

Erikson, E. H. (1963). *Childhood and society* (2nd ed.). New York: W. W. Norton.

Frankl, V. (1967). *Psychotherapy and existentialism.* New York: Washington Square Press.

Fredrickson, B. L. (2001). The role of positive emotions in positive psychology: The broaden-and-build theory of positive emotions. *American Psychologist, 56,* 218-226.

Freud, S. (1961). Jokes and their relation to the unconscious. In J. Strachey (Ed. & Trans.), *The standard edition of the complete psychological works of Sigmund Freud* (Vol. 8). London: Hogarth Press. (Original work published 1905).

Freud, S. (1961). Humour. In J. Strachey (Ed. & Trans.), *The standard edition of the complete psychological works of Sigmund Freud* (Vol. 21). London: Hogarth Press. (Original work published 1927).

Gruner, C. E. (1978). *Understanding laughter: The workings of wit and humor.* Chicago: Nelson Hall.

Harlow, H. F. (1959). Love in infant monkeys. *Scientific American, 200*(6), 67-74.

Hobbes, T. (1840). Tripos. In W. Molesworth (Ed.), *The English works of Thomas Hobbes* (Vol. 4). London: John Bohn.

Hyers, C. (1981). *The comic vision and the Christian faith.* New York: Pilgrim Press.

Keck, D. (1996). *Forgetting whose we are: Alzheimer's disease and the love of God.* Nashville: Abingdon.

Keith-Spiegel, P. (1972). Early conceptions of humor: Varieties and issues. In J. H. Goldstein & P. E. McGhee (Eds.), *The psychology of humor: Theoretical perspectives and empirical issues* (pp. 4-39). New York: Academic Press.

Kierkegaard, S. (1978). *Parables of Kierkegaard* (ed. Thomas C. Oden, p. 30). Princeton, NJ: Princeton University Press.

Kitwood, T. (1997). *Dementia reconsidered: The person comes first.* Philadelphia: Open Court Press.

Kohut, H. (1966). Forms and transformations of narcissism. *Journal of the American Psychoanalytic Association, 14,* 243-272.

Labouvie-Vief, G., & Medler, M. (2002). Affect optimization and affect complexity: Modes and styles of regulation in adulthood. *Psychology and Aging, 17,* 571-588.

Martin, R. A. (2002). Is laughter the best medicine? Humor, laughter, and physical health. *Current directions in psychological science, 11,* 216-220.

McFadden. S. H. (1999). Surprised by joy and burdened by age: The journal and letters of John Casteel. In L. E. Thomas, & S. A. Eisenhandler (Eds.), *Religion, belief, and spirituality in late life* (pp. 137-149). New York: Springer.

McFadden, S. H. (1990). Authentic humor as an expression of spiritual maturity. In J. J. Seeber (Ed.), *Spiritual maturity in the later years* (pp. 131-142). New York: The Haworth Press, Inc.

McFadden, S. H., Ingram, M., & Baldauf, C. (2000). Actions, feelings, and values: Foundations of meaning and personhood in dementia. *Journal of Religious Gerontology, 11*(3/4), 67-86.

Moody, H. R. (2002). The changing meaning of aging. In R. S. Weiss & S. A. Bass (Eds.), *Challenges of the third age: Meaning and purpose in later life* (pp. 41-54). New York: Oxford University Press.

Moody, H. R. (1986). The meaning of life and the meaning of old age. In T. R. Cole & S. A. Gadow (Eds.), *What does it mean to grow old? Reflections from the humanities* (pp. 9-40). Durham, NC: Duke University Press.

Morreall, J. (1999). *Comedy, tragedy, and religion.* Albany: State University of New York Press.

Morreall, J. (1983). *Taking laughter seriously.* Albany: State University of New York Press.

Niebuhr, R. (1969). Humor and faith. In C. Hyers (Ed.), *Holy laughter* (pp. 134-149). New York: Seabury Press.

Palmore, E. B. (1986). Attitudes toward aging shown by humor: A review. In L. Nahemow, K. A. McCluskey-Fawcett, & P. E. McGhee (Eds.), *Humor and aging* (pp. 101-119). San Diego: Academic Press.

Post, S. G. (1995). *The moral challenge of Alzheimer Disease*. Baltimore: Johns Hopkins Press.

Riley, M. W., & Riley, J. W. (1994). Structural lag: Past and future. In M. W. Riley, R. Kahn, & A. Foner (Eds.), *Age and structural lag* (pp. 15-36). New York: Wiley.

Ryff, C. D. & Singer, B. (2003). Ironies of the human condition: Well being and health on the way to mortality. In L. S. Aspinwall, & U. M. Staudinger (Eds.), *A psychology of human strengths: Fundamental questions and future directions for a positive psychology* (pp. 271-287). Washington, DC: American Psychological Association.

Saroglou, V. (2002). Religiousness, religious fundamentalism, and quest as predictors of humor creation. *International Journal for the Psychology of Religion, 12*, 177-188.

Scott-Maxwell, F. (1968). *The measure of my days*. New York: A. A. Knopf.

Seligman, M. E. P., & Peterson, C. (2003). Positive clinical psychology. In L. S. Aspinwall & U. M. Staudinger (Eds.), *A psychology of human strengths: Fundamental questions and future directions for a positive psychology* (pp. 305-317). Washington, DC: American Psychological Association.

Swabey, M. C. (1961). *Comic laughter: A philosophical essay*. New Haven: Yale University Press.

Lift Up Your Hearts:
Humour and Despair in Later Life

Heather Thomson, PhD

SUMMARY. According to Erikson, the homework of later life is integrity versus despair. The work of integrity is difficult, especially when faced with loss and grief, with the pain, suffering and anxiety that often accompany later life. However, it is also the case that humour accompanies the ageing process, and that elderly people laugh at all things associated with ageing right through to death. This paper explores the relationship between humour and despair in the task of integrity. It does so from the work of Kierkegaard, who argued that despair is a sign that we are spiritual beings. Humour comes from our responses to despair–either as giving in too easily and not attempting integrity at all, or as a willful defiance and denial of this task. Ageing humour is used to illustrate Kierkegaard's argument. Humour is then shown to function in various ways. It raises our sights when we too easily retreat into our perishing bodies. It earths us when we attempt to get too spiritual, and it

Heather Thomson teaches Systematic Theology at St. Mark's National Theological Centre, Canberra, the School of Theology for Charles Sturt University. She also teaches courses at the Centre for Ageing and Pastoral Studies (CAPS) in Canberra, and has worked as a Research Assistant for CAPS on the spiritual dimensions of ageing with dementia residents.

[Haworth co-indexing entry note]: "Lift Up Your Hearts: Humour and Despair in Later Life." Thomson, Heather. Co-published simultaneously in *Journal of Religious Gerontology* (The Haworth Pastoral Press, an imprint of The Haworth Press, Inc.) Vol. 16, No. 3/4, 2004, pp. 29-41; and: *Spirituality of Later Life: On Humor and Despair* (ed: Rev. Elizabeth MacKinlay) The Haworth Pastoral Press, an imprint of The Haworth Press, Inc., 2004, pp. 29-41. Single or multiple copies of this article are available for a fee from The Haworth Document Delivery Service [1-800-HAWORTH, 9:00 a.m. - 5:00 p.m. (EST). E-mail address: docdelivery@haworthpress.com].

gives us a glimpse of the larger framework of God's future out of which we are invited to live, and to "lift up our hearts." *[Article copies available for a fee from The Haworth Document Delivery Service: 1-800-HAWORTH. E-mail address: <docdelivery@haworthpress.com> Website: <http://www. HaworthPress.com>* © 2004 by The Haworth Press, Inc. All rights reserved.]

KEYWORDS. Humour, ageing, spirituality, despair, theology, laughter, God

As I have turned my theological interests to the area of ageing and spirituality over the past few years, I have brought with me my interest in humour. When you have an eye or an ear for humour it is surprising where you find it–and it definitely accompanies those who age. I have been studying humour for some time now, and enjoy the insights it gives. I like humour's creativity and its attitude, its ability to transcend a situation, and its sheer fun, and for what it says about the human spirit. We are the only animals who laugh, and to me, humour is like dancing or like jazz–which other animals can't do either. It rides above a situation, plays on top of things, brings us down to earth when we try to be angels, and takes us out of being caught in the ordinary with our heads down. At its best, humour is inspirational and challenging and energetic and life giving–in short it is a spiritual exercise.

When I began to work with Elizabeth MacKinlay in researching ageing and spirituality, I came to realise that Elizabeth shares an interest in humour also, derived from her studies and interviews with elderly people. So it seemed good the Holy Spirit and to us to plan this conference around the theme of humour and despair in later life.

In Erikson's stages of human development he names the final stage as integrity versus despair (Erikson et al., 1986). Integrity is the challenge of later life. When faced with illness and pain, loss of powers and functions, loss of friends and relatives, can we nevertheless retain integrity around a certain trust and faith in life, in God? Or will we lose that basic trust and hope, and fall into despair?

Despair is not the same as depression or sadness, or feeling down. It is all right to feel sad, depressed or grief-stricken over losses encountered in later life, in fact it is good and healthy to do so. But these are usually temporary–a stage to go through. Despair is a more pervasive attitude to a situation, or to life in general. It is not so much about a particular loss or grief. It is totalising. It is a lack of faith and hope that things could ever be any better. It is a total loss of hope, and as such, is a matter not just of feelings but of the spirit.

My interest in humour comes in part from despair, particularly a study of despair by the Danish philosopher, Soren Kierkegaard (1941). He argues that the fact that human beings fall into despair is a sign that we are spiritual beings. And the way we respond to despair is the source of Humour. So in my mind, if we can better understand despair and humour, this might serve us in the process of integrity in later life.

In another paper in this collection of essays Susan McFadden helpfully addresses despair from a psychological point of view. Here we are adding to that by looking at despair as a matter of spirit. Kierkegaard says that human life is a balancing act. This is well illustrated by a cartoon of a tightrope walker by an Australian cartoonist, Michael Leunig (1997). Here we see a little man on a unicycle balancing on a rope high above the earth. One end of the rope is tied to a cloud, the other is held up by a bird. It is a delightful picture, a picture of the impossible yet he is achieving the balance with the help of a balancing beam, and feeling pretty good about it.

Although we are finite earth creatures, this cartoon depicts our infinite hopes and desires. We belong both to the temporal and the eternal. We are part of the world of necessity–including the laws of physics and chemistry and gravity and time–and part of the world of possibility. We have the ability to transcend the immediate moment, and to create new possibilities that have not existed before. Human beings are this strange and incongruous mix of finite and infinite, temporal and eternal, bound and free (Kierkegaard 1941).

However, being human is a balancing act in which we don't always succeed. Leunig's cartoon has more to it. When you look on the next page you see a little man face down in the grass. Beside him is a bent unicycle and broken balancing beam. The tightrope walker has fallen to the ground. One tends to smile at the first cartoon, but laugh at the second, when he comes a cropper. Kierkegaard sees humour in not getting our balancing act right. That is what makes us laughable.

The work of integrity is to see this incongruous mixture that we are as the potential through which we become a self before God, or as Kierkegaard says, a "spirit." For this is our calling. It is eternity's demand, or invitation, to us. If we *fail* in this integrity, fail to live within the limits and possibilities of being human, then we are, in his terms "infinitely comic" (1941, 154)–not so much funny, as ridiculous.

There are two sides to this failure to be integrated. On the one hand, we may fail to accept that we are earth-bound, finite, mortal creatures. Then we would live our lives in the clouds, trying to escape our lot. We would be disconnected from real, day-to-day life, and from our bodies, chasing our own heads. Michael Leunig has another cartoon that illustrates this, of a man chasing his own head with a butterfly net. He has allowed his head to get away from him, to be disconnected from his earth-bound body.

On the other hand, if we accept that we are of the earth, and are limited by time and gravity, yet fail to lift up our heads above the flux and see ourselves also as spirits, then what makes us different from the sheep and the cattle? A Gary Larson cartoon shows this aspect of being human. He draws a flock of sheep all grazing with their heads down, except for one sheep that is standing up saying, "Hey. Listen to me. We don't have to be just sheep." Integrity means knowing our place *between* heaven and earth, not entirely with the other animals, and not entirely out of this world.

For Kierkegaard, when we fail to become ourselves, "spirits," conscious of being constituted by God, and of living before God, then we fall into despair (1941, 59-60). But for him, being aware of despair is not something that is depressing. On the contrary, he sees it as uplifting and inspiring, for it views each of us through the lens of eternity's demand on us, that we be spirit (1941, 155). Despair is a sign that we belong to eternity as well as to the earth.

When people fall into despair, which we all do from time to time, there are two common reactions to it, and these each relate to different ways of being comic, or ridiculous. One common reaction to despair is *weakness* or avoidance, not willing to even try being an integrated self. It would mean, in Leunig's second cartoon, remaining on the grass and never trying to tightrope walk again. In the face of difficulties, some people, he says, just swoon and lie down and play dead (1941, 186).

George Burns said this about growing old. When he was 93 he observed that many people as they approach old age just give in, whereas he saw age as a state of mind, an attitude. He said,

> I see people that the minute they get to be 65, start rehearsing to be old. They start taking little steps, they practice grunting when they sit down . . . they drop food on themselves, they take little naps when you're talking to them, and by the time they get to be seventy, they've made it . . . they're now old. (1984, 131)

George Burns made sure he kept company with younger people. He didn't think it was good when older people just hung around each other comparing gravy stains (1996, 291).

So, one reaction to despair is weakness, or giving in. The second reaction is *defiance*, a see-if-I-care attitude that confirms oneself where one is and defiantly refuses to change. Such a person is revolting against existence, as if his or her life was proof against the goodness of existence. Kierkegaard illustrates this with a story. Suppose a writer makes a typographical error on the page. The writer goes to erase the error, but the error comes to life. It says to the writer, "No, I will not be erased. I will stand as a witness against you, that you are a very poor writer" (1941, 207). This attitude is defiance in error, and some people live their lives that way. They do not want to change or to come to terms with bad experiences, but live their lives in their damaged form as a testimony that the powers that be must be bad.

Many people enter their later years of life with a lot of baggage. They are travelling heavily loaded, full of resentments and bitterness and anger, but they won't let go, because they want to live as a testimony that they have been hard done by. They want to prove that they are the victims of particular people or powers in their lives, who have treated them badly. The film, "Grumpy Old Men," epitomises such characters.

The point is, to remain like this, for the rest of their lives, is a form of defiance in error. It is a reaction to despair but a ridiculous reaction because it denies that they could and should move on and make something of themselves. It denies eternity in the self. No matter what has happened in one's life, the question remains for each of us, how shall I live this part of my life well?

How we deal with despair is the question, and humour comes from the more ridiculous ways that we try to avoid, by weakness or defiance, our spiritual task of integrity. By turning our attention now to humour about ageing, we will see that humour can serve us in the process of integrity. It does so, I believe, in three ways:

1. Humour earths us when we think we are too important, or too sexy to be the finite, temporal, mortal creatures that we are. A lot of ageing humour is very earthy.
2. Humour laughs at the ridiculous ways in which we fail, by weakness or defiance, to become integrated selves. In this regard, Kierkegaard believes that we need a good doctrine of original sin to understand humour.

3. Humour takes us out of our finitude and mortality to see ourselves in a larger picture, where the joke is not on us, but for us. Christian theology holds to the resurrection as God's joke against finitude and death, and invites us to "lift up our hearts."

I will expand on each of these further in relation to ageing humour.

1. HUMOUR EARTHS US

I have heard that inside every older person there is a younger person–wondering what the hell happened! Time continues on its relentless journey, and we are carried along with it whether we like it or not. Some ageing humour is about the ride of life, and it reminds us there is no getting off.

Jerry Seinfeld likens life to a ride:

Life is truly a ride. We're all strapped in and no one can stop it . . . As you make each passage from youth to adulthood to maturity, sometimes you put your hands up and scream, sometimes you just hang on to the bar in front of you . . . I think the most you can hope for at the end of life is that your hair's messed, you're out of breath, and you didn't throw up. (1993, 153)

My father used another metaphor for the passage of time. Rather than a ride, he likened the life span to a day. Childhood was early morning, mid life was midday. You get the picture? So by the time he was turning 50 he was in the mid afternoon of his life, at 60, the later afternoon, at 70 he was in the early evening. We used to ask him, "Are you working on Daylight Saving Time, Dad, or Eastern Standard time? Because if you're on Eastern Standard Time, it's not long before curtains." He would wander off mumbling *something* about bloody kids.

Regarding time, there is a lot of ageing humour that tries to mark the turning point from temporary youth to middle or old age. George Burns said, "You know you're getting old when you stoop to tie you shoelaces and you ask yourself, what else can I do while I'm down here?" (*Oh My Aging Funny Bone*).

Others say they suddenly become appalled by the way that modern mirrors distort the reflection, or they are amazed when they hang something in the wardrobe for a while and it shrinks two sizes.

Apart from those moments of realisation that one has progressed into later life, there are specific themes that are treated with humour as a way of earthing us, reminding us of our decaying bodies, falling flesh, lower sex drives and looming death. As Bette Davis put it, "Old age ain't no place for sissies" (*Oh My Aging Funny Bone*).

One book on ageing humour is called, *Falling Flesh Just Ahead: And Other Signs on the Road Towards Midlife* (Potts 1998). Gravity takes its toll. And our bodies just wear out. I've seen a cartoon of a young man walking along the street with a T-shirt on saying, "I climbed Mount Everest." Beside him is an old man walking along with a T-shirt saying, "I climbed out of bed." George Burns, still performing in his 90s, said "I get a standing ovation just standing." Bob Hope, when he was 80 played up the stereotype. "I don't feel 80," he said. "In fact I don't feel *anything* until noon. And then it's time for my nap" (Metcalf 1987, 181).

This sort of humour reminds us of our reduced capacities and powers in later life, and of our resultant lowering of expectations. I have an example of such humour from a dementia resident in an aged care facility, from a CAPS research project that I was involved with. During a weekly discussion group of dementia patients, the diversional therapist was summing up one day, and asked the residents, "What about now. Would you say that you are happy now?" One man thought for a while and said, "Well, I took a suppository this morning." We began to laugh at this reduction of happiness to bodily functions. He knew exactly what he was saying, and smiling added, "Well, I needed it." We laughed more, and his timing was perfect–he grinned broadly and said, "And it worked."

Ageing humour gets very earthy when it deals with questions of continence and sex. And yet, awful as it is to experience loss of powers in these areas of life, we would probably all know jokes about them. It is part of the incongruity of being earth creatures, yet spiritual beings, made to the image and likeness of God. It just doesn't seem to fit together sometimes, and what we often think of as the glory of being human gets reduced down to whether or not we can go to the toilet when we want to.

My father told me the following joke–he thought it was hilarious. Three men were discussing ageing in a nursing home. One said, "I have trouble peeing. I wake every morning at 7 am and I stand at the toilet and I want to pee but I can't. Nothing comes out." The second man said, "I have trouble crapping. I wake at 8 am and I feel that I want to go, but I can't seem to do it. I take laxatives, I eat bran–it won't shift me." The third man says, "That's nothing. I pee every morning at 7. No problem.

Then I crap at 8. Every day without fail." "So what's your problem?" asked the second man. "Well," said the third, "I don't wake up till 9."

Does joking about bodily functions prepare us, perhaps, for when it is our turn, or is it a way of keeping it at a distance, something that is happening to others over there and not to me? It is probably both. The comic contrast is between the way a person used to be when they were young compared with when they are old. There is also a contrast between able-bodied people now and the present aged population, not quite in control of their powers.

It is a similar situation with humour about sex. This could be entitled "the spirit is willing but the flesh is just too damn tired" (Stott 1994). George Burns, who lived to nearly 100, had a few things to say on this subject. He said in his later life, "I'm at that age when just putting my cigar in its holder is a thrill" (Metcalf 1987, 180). He is also reported to have said, "having sex at 90 is like trying to shoot pool with a rope." And I think that's pretty sad for all of us, don't you?

I have heard success stories too–jokes bragging about what was achieved by someone who others might have thought were "past it." But let's move on. As well as the ageing body as the subject of much Humour, there is also the ageing mind. Humour is found in real-life situations when grandma or grandpa puts their shoes away in the fridge, or they get themselves dressed with their underpants on their head. I know of families who do their best to treat such family members well and with respect in these circumstances, but when they are out of hearing, the rest of the family laugh until the tears roll down. It is the comic (and tragic) clash between this person as they are now, and as they were in the past, when they had their full mind. It is also a comic clash is between this family member's behaviour, and that which is considered normal in present society.

I recently saw a joke about the ageing mind.

> Three sisters lived together, aged 92, 94, and 96. One night the 96-year-old runs a bath. She puts her foot in and pauses. She yells down the stairs, "Was I getting in or out of the bath?"
>
> The 94-year-old yells back, "I don't know, I'll come up and see." She starts up the stairs and pauses. "Was I going up the stairs or down?"
>
> The 92-year-old is sitting at the kitchen table having tea listening to her sisters. She shakes her head and says, "I sure hope I never get that forgetful." She knocks on wood for good measure.

Then she yells "I'll come and help both of you as soon as I see who's at the door." (*Oh My Aging Funny Bone*)

Another way that humour keeps us grounded is to remind us of death and the afterlife, and that whether we like it or not, we will not find integrity until we come to terms with our own death. Some humour just makes light of the whole thing. I have heard, for example, that for three days after death, hair and fingernails continue to grow, but phone calls taper off (Metcalf 1987, 69). I have also seen a tombstone at Narooma on the NSW south Coast that says, "See, I told you I was sick."

Some humour is about trying to deny death. Woody Allen is good at expressing fear of death. He said that he doesn't mind dying; he just doesn't want to be there when it happens. He also said that he doesn't believe in an afterlife, although he is bringing a change of underwear. Whatever our response to thinking about death, the question remains whether we, or it, will have the last laugh. Christian theology has a position on this, but we will get to that in a minute.

This section has looked at the way humour functions to keep us earth-bound when we think we can escape our lot in some way. It will not let us pretend to be angels, or to forget that we have bodies that wear out and disappoint us in one way or another, and will eventually die. That is what we have to come to terms with as one aspect of our spiritual task of ageing.

2. HUMOUR LAUGHS AT OUR WEAKNESS AND DEFIANCE IN RESPONSE TO AGING

The second way in which humour can help us discern the spiritual tasks of ageing is by showing how ridiculous it is to avoid the questions at all. Some people tend to lie down and play dead in the face of old age, or defiantly pretend that it is not happening. Nancy Astor said "I refuse to admit that I am more than 52, even if that makes my sons illegitimate" (Metcalf 1987, 12).

Perhaps this area of humour is best summarised in a quote by Catherine Aird. "If you can't be a good example, then you'll just have to be a horrible warning" (*Psycho Proverb Zone*). This is where grumpy old men come into their own–as a warning to the rest of us not to go down that track. They waste so much time trying to get back at the other person, or settling old scores, that they don't get on with living and enjoying what they do have.

One way in which people become a horrible warning is through plastic surgery, a topic alluded to in other papers. Humour latches on to the ridiculousness of such measures. I heard of a woman, for example, who had so many bottom-lifts that she ended up with a head-rest. George Burns has a whole chapter in one of his books on cosmetic surgery, and marvels about what can be done, to so many parts of the body, inside and out, to replace or hide the effects of ageing. Then he says,

> I went out the other night with an attractive girl who told me she was 20. Later I found out I was dancing with a 70-year-old man. I'm not well. I should have guessed when she told me her name was Irving. (Burns 1984, 120)

This is an example of defiance in error, defiantly trying to stay young, and the comedians show how ludicrous it is.

Those who try to deny getting older often take up with the younger generation. This in itself is not a bad thing, but I am thinking of Groucho Marx, who I am led to believe was a bit of a grouch in his later life, and preferred the company of younger women. He said, "A man's only as old as the woman he feels" (Metcalf 1987, 181). It is a clever and witty remark, but it is also a denial of aging.

At times ageing is associated positively with wisdom. But sometimes ageing comes along all by itself. Instead of wisdom we see unresolved anger and resentment. A number of comedy sketches of older people portray them as cunning and manipulative, under the guise of the little old helpless lady or man. The Australian comedy called "Mother and Son" showed the aged mother this way. It was hilarious to watch her outwit her poor, unsuspecting middle-aged son who cared for her, but you wouldn't wish her on anyone. This is the comedy that comes from the willful refusal to become an integrated, responsible self. We laugh because we know it to be a ridiculous way to live, especially for people who are way past having grown up in a chronological sense, and who, you would think, may have learned by now to do better.

Humour functions here to laugh at those who take the bitter and twisted road into old age, or the weak or defiant, for it intuits the comic clash between their path and the one they should be on, the path towards integrity and living one's life well before God.

3. HUMOUR POINTS US TO FREEDOM AND POSSIBILITY

The third way in which humour helps us on the road to integrity is to remind us of possibilities and freedoms that we may have forgotten, in being so caught up in daily life and perhaps suffering. While the first kind of humour earthed us, this humour lifts up our minds and our hearts. It tells us, we don't have to be just sheep.

Noel Coward has a nice little verse that illustrates this. Speaking of growing old gracefully, he introduces us to Elsie, aged 74. She says it is first a question of being sincere, and next, if you are supple you have nothing to fear,

> Then she swung upside down on a glass chandelier,
> I couldn't have liked it more. (Metcalf 1987, 180)

This type of humour delights in the freedoms and possibilities that we do have, limited as they may be. It is not backward looking and regretful, but forward-looking and hopeful.

I have a photograph of myself on my mantle-piece from the time we were first married. We lived at Bronte Beach in Sydney, and I was walking back from the beach with a towel over my shoulder, wearing what my husband refers to as a rather fetching one-piece swimming costume. I look at this photo nostalgically as the woman I used to be. Recently I was telling a friend and colleague about this, regretting the signs of ageing that I would not fit into my fetching one-piece these days, and he exercised the ministry of admonition. He told me off. A Christian point of view, he said, is not backward looking, but forward looking. Instead of thinking about the woman I used to be, I should be spending my time and energy on the woman I am becoming. I should be living for, and out of, the future.

I put this view to the conference committee, and suggested that we have T-shirts made saying, "The woman (or man) I am becoming" across the front. We all thought it was a good idea, but we ran out of time and energy to do it. Nevertheless, we have now passed on the idea, and you can have one made yourself if you wish. It is quite a different perspective on life.

Ultimately, this third kind of humour relies on a basic trust and faith that the world is not a joke against us but is a divine joke, which is for us. It relies on faith in God, whose "greatest stunt of all" was the resurrection, where life won out over death, possibility over tragic necessity (Echardt 1995, 134-5). In the light of this, we can let go clinging to the perishable things of the world, and lighten our load. We are free to laugh at all things human, all pretensions to glory and power, and are free not to take anything human ultimately seriously.

Clowning fits into this type of humour. Clowns don't take anything too seriously. They wear funny clothes, making us wonder about the clothes we wear and how we invest them sometimes with too much importance and prestige. They do seemingly impossible tricks, like Leunig's tightrope walker. And clowns play. Play and humour, are what Peter Berger (1997) calls intimations of transcendence–that ultimately the victory has been won, all will be well, and we need not get ourselves caught in the deadly serious.

Although we cannot minimise the real loss, tragedy and suffering experienced in later life, we can hold also to a hopefulness that what happens in this perishable world does not have the final word. One theologian put it this way.

> We never did ask to be born. Neither do we ask to be subjected to Death, the final insult and final evil *vis-à-vis* Life . . . To many persons, here is grievous cause for pessimism . . . Yet to others, the door stays open, if only barely ajar, to a salvation wrought by God. (Echardt 1995, 134-5)

In thinking about humour and despair in later life, we have seen how humour can serve us in the spiritual tasks of ageing. humour reminds us of our animal natures, and that even though we may be a little less than God, we have to live with physical weaknesses, embarrassments, inconveniences, and rude interruptions, with ageing and death. On the other hand, humour lifts up our sights if we settle for being just sheep, and gives us a glimpse of possibilities that do exist, and that call us ever forward. And humour plays a part in getting us back on the tightrope when we fall off, so that we might again try to integrate the call of earth and the call of heaven upon us.

In Christian terms, humour helps us to love both our relation to earth and to heaven, for it knows the folly of trying to deny one or the other. And humour testifies to the creativity and possibilities of being human, in such a way that it is itself a sign of our relation to God. Just as despair is a sign that we are spiritual beings, so is humour.

So, lift up your hearts. Live out of the future, and keep the door open, if only barely ajar, to the salvation wrought by God.

REFERENCES

Berger, P. (1997). *Redeeming Laughter: The Comic Dimension of Human Experience.* New York: Walter De Gruyter.

Burns, G. (1984). *How to Live to be 100–or More.* London: Robson Books.

Burns, G. (1996). *The Hundred Year Dash.* New York: Simon & Schuster.

Echardt, A.R. (1995). *How to Tell God From the Devil.* New Brunswick: Transaction.

Erikson, E.H., Erikson, J.M. and Kivnick, H.Q. (1986). *Vital Involvement in Old Age.* New York: W. W. Norton & Co.

Kierkegaard, S. (1941). "The Sickness Unto Death," in *Fear and Trembling and The Sickness unto Death.* Trans. Walter Lowrie, New York: Double Day.

Kuschel, K-J. (1994). *Laughter: A Theological Reflection.* London: SCM Press.

Leunig, M. (1974). *A Penguin Leunig.* Middlesex: Penguin Books.

Metcalf, F. (ed) (1987). *The Penguin Dictionary of Modern Humorous Quotations.* London: Penguin Books.

Potts, L. (1998). *Falling Flesh Just Ahead: And Other Signs on the Road Towards Midlife.* Atlanta: Longstreet Press.

Seinfeld, J. (1993). *SeinLanguage.* New York: Bantam Books.

Web Sites

Oh My Aging Funny Bone
http://www.seniorresource.com/jokes.htm

Psycho Proverb Zone: Catherine Aird
http://proverb.taiwanonline.org/display.php?author=Catherine+Aird&row=0

Humour:
A Way to Transcendence in Later Life?

Elizabeth MacKinlay, PhD, RN

SUMMARY. This paper outlines connections between humour and self-transcendence in later life. Self-transcendence is described as a spiritual task of ageing. Material illustrating transcendence of disabilities and energy lack is drawn from in-depth interviews of older people, living independently and in residential aged care. The journey to spiritual integrity is proposed as a spiritual process that older people may engage in and humour is suggested as a means to that process. Connections are made between disability and loss and the capacity for self-transcendence in later life. *[Article copies available for a fee from The Haworth Document Delivery Service: 1-800-HAWORTH. E-mail address: <docdelivery@ haworthpress.com> Website: <http://www.HaworthPress.com> © 2004 by The Haworth Press, Inc. All rights reserved.]*

KEYWORDS. Humour, ageing, transcendence, spirituality, spiritual integrity

---

Elizabeth MacKinlay is Director, Centre for Ageing and Pastoral Studies, and Associate Professor, School of Theology, Charles Sturt University, 15 Blackall Street, Barton, ACT 2600, Australia (E-mail: emackinlay@csu.edu.au).

[Haworth co-indexing entry note]: "Humour: A Way to Transcendence in Later Life?" MacKinlay, Elizabeth. Co-published simultaneously in *Journal of Religious Gerontology* (The Haworth Pastoral Press, an imprint of The Haworth Press, Inc.) Vol. 16, No. 3/4, 2004, pp. 43-58; and: *Spirituality of Later Life: On Humor and Despair* (ed: Rev. Elizabeth MacKinlay) The Haworth Pastoral Press, an imprint of The Haworth Press, Inc., 2004, pp. 43-58. Single or multiple copies of this article are available for a fee from The Haworth Document Delivery Service [1-800-HAWORTH, 9:00 a.m. - 5:00 p.m. (EST). E-mail address: docdelivery@haworthpress.com].

http://www.haworthpress.com/web/JRG
© 2004 by The Haworth Press, Inc. All rights reserved.
Digital Object Identifier: 10.1300/J078v16n03_04

Is there a spiritual component in humour? Is laughter part of the spiritual dimension? These were questions I asked, while analysing the stories of older people from in-depth interviews of where these people found meaning in life. When I studied the transcripts of the in-depth interviews, humour was expressed naturally in many of their stories. I want to make it clear that when I began my studies I did not seek to find instances of humour. This is one of the benefits of a qualitative method of study, as I was able to discover things that were happening for these older people that might not have been shown through the use of questionnaire alone. I will come back to their stories and humour later in this paper.

In this paper, I will explore the place of humour in human transcendence in later life. First, I want to look briefly at some of the literature on humour, then examine transcendence as a spiritual task of ageing and humour as a means to self-transcendence. At the same time, I do not want to paint a picture of ageing that is all fun and laughter. That would be to deny the reality of some of the experiences in later life that include not only joy and laughter, but sadness and pain. Psychosocial development in ageing has been described by Erikson (1986), as a stage where a certain tension continues between the movement towards integrity, or towards the other side of the continuum of psychosocial development in later life, characterised by despair. These experiences of life are echoed through the Psalms, filled with the repertoire of human experiences, from laughter, joy and triumph, to suffering, pain and despair.

Penelope Wilcock, in a chapter titled *The Caged Bird*, writes of the importance of Humour as a tool of healing for those who have had a stroke (2004). Wilcock also remarks that in the depth of depression following a stroke, humour may seem to desert the person. She sees the ability to laugh at some of the indignities of stroke as a 'healing milestone.' humour and laughter are closely linked, however, laughter and humour can each occur separately (Lefcourt and Martin, 1986). Commonly, humour is understood as the functioning of rather complex higher order cognitive-emotional processes, while laughter is understood as a reflex-like physiological-behavioural response. Like crying, humour and laughter may have a number of meanings and functions. While humour can be used to mock, ridicule, or coerce, it may also be a means of reducing interpersonal tensions and 'expressing a feeling of oneness with others and the universe' (Lefcourt, 1986, p. 4).

Humour that occurs in situations that would normally elicit a negative response, such as sadness or fear, was one of three categories of Humour referred to by Freud (in Lefcourt, 1986). In such situations humour, leading to laughter allows an altered perspective, and results in avoiding the negative consequences of the situation. 'The laughter of humour arises from the release of energy that would have been associated with this painful emotion but has now become redundant' (p. 6).

Another way of looking at the use of humour, and perhaps more relevant, from a spiritual perspective, is found in Frankl's work (1984, p. 63). Frankl writes that humour is one of the 'soul's weapons in the fight for self-preservation.' Here, speaking of the soul, it seems that humour is at the core of the struggle for existence, humour can become a strength when one has one's back to the wall. Frankl writes out of some of the experiences of humour, in the most difficult of World War 2 concentration camp settings. In the 1997 edition of Frankl's *Man's Search for Ultimate Meaning*, he wrote of 'two uniquely human capacities of self-transcendence and self-detachment' (1997, p. 110). According to Frankl, a technique called paradoxical intention may be used to distance the person from their problem, by 'a unique and specific aspect of self-detachment, namely, the human sense of humour' (p. 110). It is said that in laughing at the problem it distances, and diffuses the topic, 'takes the wind out of the sails' (Frankl, 1986, pp. 224-5).

An everyday example using humour by distancing, is where an older person laughs or jokes at their decreasing mobility, or their forgetfulness, as in the commonly used expression-'a senior moment.' This move comes from within the person; it is not making a joke at someone else's expense. Jokes that emphasise the negative aspects of ageing may be offensive to some older people, yet on the other hand older people may use such stories of failing health against themselves, initiating a humorous anecdote. This has been noticeable in some of the small spiritual reminiscence groups of people who have dementia and are in residential aged care. The following is a short conversation between a couple of people, who were participants in one of these small groups.

> First resident: . . . "there is a word I am looking for but I can't remember it, that is one of my problems finding the words. As you get older you know you find it more difficult."
>
> Second resident: "You need a dictionary."
>
> First resident: "Yes, by the time you have found it in there you have lost interest."

It is interesting that people in the small groups engaged in conversations around memory loss, and laughed about it, however, it is noted that in the above exchange, memory loss was identified as part of growing older, not dementia. Behind the jokes may lie a fear of memory loss and its possible implications. Thus the use of humour to distance oneself from the feared situation may act to lessen its impact. We have found in our studies a stigma attached to the word 'dementia' (MacKinlay, Trevitt, and Hobart, 2002) and a reluctance to participate in our groups where we used the word 'dementia.' We had more people willing to take part in the studies where we used the term 'memory loss.'

Similar in effect are the superiority theories of humour that claim we laugh at others less able than ourselves, or at other people's misfortunes. Humour of this type can have the effect of distancing or dissociation from the situation. Humour may also be directed at one's self; it is possible to laugh at one's own misfortunes, resulting in enhanced feelings of self-esteem and mastery, thus threats to the self can lose their power and be dismissed. Alternatively, laughing at one's own misfortune may be a sign of transcendence of the misfortune. Lefcourt and Martin (1986) found in their study that humour touches on matters of great profundity in the human condition.

Yet another group of theories of humour are the incongruity theories. These focus on the way in which humour alters the person's perception of the situation, making the situation less stressful and therefore less arousing (Lefcourt, 1986). Again, as with Frankl's paradoxical intention, the situation is defused, producing a healthy response to tension raising situations. Could this be why Sarah laughed when, she heard from the Lord, that, in her later life, when she thought she was too old for child bearing, she was to be a mother? (Gen 18).

We may think of the comedy show of an older woman and her son on television, titled *Mother and Son*. The mother, Maggie, always got her way in the end. Often the laughter occurred in response to Maggie's actions, like trying to remember in what part of the garden they had scattered her late husband's ashes, and then trying to dig them up-were his ashes under the rose bush? Or, when at the cemetery, the large bag of oranges Maggie was carrying suddenly spilling out into the open grave. At other times the plight of her unfortunate son was the source of laughter. Perhaps Maggie had dementia, it is left unstated in the show, and the viewer is left wondering, did Maggie really know what she was doing, was she manipulating her son, or did she not have insight into her behaviour? This show treated issues of ageing and perhaps dementia in a humorous way that helped to bring these sensitive issues into the open.

However, some people have found it too hard to watch that TV show, for them it seemed too close to reality, and not funny at all!

An important aspect of the Lefcourt and Martin findings was the 'value of acceptance and forgiveness of one's self and others that is inherent in humour' (1986, p. 124). Where this occurs, it becomes possible to let go and move beyond and transcend the situation.

> To laugh with someone about what would seem to be an alien anguish is to know that anguish as a surrogate for one's own familiar pains; and the humour that results is perceivable as one shared 'victimhood'-the state of our species all too aware of its own mortality. (Lefcourt and Martin, 1986, p. 126)

There is a delicate distinction to be made between laughing with and laughing at; the laughing with enables connection with the other, laughing at serves to alienate the other.

HUMOUR AND SPIRITUAL MATURITY

Is humour in ageing an outcome of spiritual maturity? (See McFadden's article in this collection of essays.) Or is it a process by which one arrives at maturity? McFadden (1990) suggests that the ability to laugh or smile in response to a situation requires both the ability to stand back from the situation, and to be 'utterly immersed' in the situation. She writes that humour can thus be considered an expression of spiritual maturity. Perhaps a sense of humour is really needed to enable older people to deal with some of the difficulties they encounter in ageing. Further, authentic humour of the spiritually mature person is acknowledged as conveying a deep sense of trust and hope.

It is important for carers working with older adults to recognise authentic humour in those they work with, and to also learn to use humour appropriately in their own work. Inappropriate use of humour appears condescending and demeaning, 'putting down' the older person. It may even be possible to devalue authentic humour; not recognising that it is a sign of the spiritual dimension.

Spiritual maturity among older people varies greatly, as with people at any age; some older persons have a deeply developed spiritual dimension, while others have focused more on physical and/or psychosocial aspects of life and come to later life with few spiritual strategies. Spiritual maturity is always a becoming, never an arrival and completion. In my studies based on the stories of older people, I set out a definition of spiritual integrity that seems to be similar to the concept of spiritual maturity. I want to propose the concept of spiritual integrity as a jumping off point for the exploration of spirituality and humour in later life. In my doctoral work with elderly people, I defined spiritual integrity as:

> a state where an individual shows by their life example and attitudes, a sense of peace with themselves and others, and development of wholeness of being. The search for meaning and a degree of transcendence is evident. (MacKinlay, 2001a, p. 180)

I am suggesting that transcendence is an important component of the spiritual journey.

In a model of spiritual tasks and process of ageing, (MacKinlay 2001a) one of the main tasks was drawn from the theme of self-sufficiency versus perceived (future) vulnerability that was expressed by so many of the independent older people. One hundred percent of those independent living older people feared future vulnerability (MacKinlay 2001a). The spiritual task drawn from this theme is transcendence of disability and loss. Varying degrees of transcendence were identified among the frail older nursing home residents (MacKinlay, 2001b). This latter group has already had to deal with multiple losses and difficulties. Vulnerability was no longer a perceived future vulnerability, it was real and now. Of this group, 45% expressed some fears, a much lower proportion than those living independently (100%). In fact, 55% said they had no fears. Even so, with 45% stating they had some fears, this is an area that needs addressing through spiritual care. The group who were fearful had not reached any marked degree of transcendence, while those who said they were not fearful had a sense of transcendence, thus fitting with the definition that with spiritual integrity, the person has a sense of peace, and is moving towards transcendence.

In a pilot study just completed of spiritual reminiscence work in people with dementia, humour could be seen as a means of transcending many of the hard parts of life (MacKinlay, Trevitt, and Hobart, 2002). Thus, one of the spiritual tasks of the process of ageing is transcendence and *humour may be a way into transcendence*. Humour may be both a means of working towards transcendence and the outcome of transcendence. It is only when one can move beyond the self, as in self-forgetting proposed by Frankl (1985) that transcendence is possible. To some extent, it is only when this occurs that humour and laughter are possible. But, also, to some extent, humour may assist in self-forgetting (Figure 1). The process of self-forgetting allows the individual to see ultimate meaning, even in and through loss and disability.

HUMOUR IN THE SHARING OF SPIRITUAL REMINISCENCE

In the first study (MacKinlay, 2001a), in a number of in-depth interviews, the informant would spontaneously laugh. I also found that quite often both informant and I, as the interviewer, would laugh together, spontaneously. It seemed to be a kind of empathetic response, and not always in the context of funny situations. A number of the instances of laughter were quite sensitive episodes, involving dying, or other situations where something had gone very wrong. There were a number of instances of laughter where the informant was recounting an anecdote and laughing at the memory, particularly of things they had done as children.

HUMOUR AS A CONNECTING POINT FOR INTIMACY

First, could humour be used to connect with others, to establish a time of intimacy with another person? (where intimacy means to be known and accepted at the deepest level). Flora (MacKinlay, 2001a) seemed initially to be testing; was it alright to have done what she was now sharing with me? Speaking of her late husband, she said:

> If something upsets me I talk to his photograph, (laughs) you know, so I think, well I must have faith in something, I mean, you don't just talk to a photograph, do you? I mean you know I really think I'm talking to him.

Flora was sharing something very personal and intimate and she laughed as she shared. This incident centred on her reflection of a habit of talking to her husband's photo. I sensed she was unsure how I would respond to her behaviour, and her laughter seemed almost to ask for affirmation from me. Would I laugh too? In this instance it didn't seem appropriate for me to laugh, it was too sensitive. She paused for a long time after sharing that with me. She seemed to be comfortable with what she had shared and then went on to share more deeply about her faith and life journey. Later in the interview, Flora joked about her fear of getting dementia:

Now talking to friends of my own age I think we all end up, we
have a dread, you know when we can't think of something, either
somebody's name or a word you can't think of, we all say or we
say, oh the old "alkaselzer's" coming on, we all dread it. (Mac-
Kinlay, 2001a, p. 194)

Flora used this story as a way of dealing with something that is often
feared. It allowed her to talk about it, and seemed to ease the tension. In
this instance Flora and interviewer laughed together about something
they hope will never happen to either of them. In these two examples,
there is an important distinction between laughing at and laughing with.
In the first instance, I could not enter into Flora's feelings for her husband; these were intimate and her own. I sensed I could not laugh then;
it would not be appropriate. I also sensed she wanted affirmation from
me, although she laughed. My response was simply to wait and be present to her. In the second example, where I did feel it was appropriate to
laugh, I was able to laugh with Flora. This use of humour can be seen as
a naturally occurring paradoxical intention, as used therapeutically by

FIGURE 1. Self-transcendence and humour: A spiritual process related to life
meaning

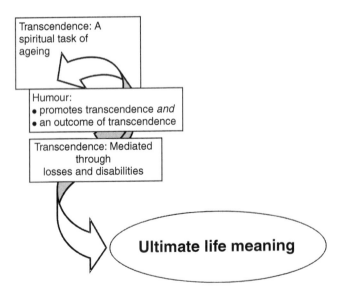

Frankl and others following him. Incidentally, Flora told me she had a suicide plan should she receive a diagnosis of Alzheimer's disease. (MacKinlay, 2001a), so beneath her laughter, there lurked fear and perhaps the potential for fear that she too would get Alzheimer's (Flora had cared for her mother who had Alzheimer's).

Carol was one of the informants in the study of independent living older people (1998), who lived with a number of chronic physical and disabling conditions. She existed on limited means, and she had a wonderful sense of humour. She told an anecdote about her problems of worrying that she would not have enough money to pay for her funeral:

> ... so she (social worker) explained to me that I could have what used to be called a "pauper's" funeral, (laughs) Oh I laughed, and I wrote a story and it starts off, "well I'm heading for the pauper's grave" and I put all the reasons why I was heading for a pauper's grave. So I sort of likened myself to Forrest Gump, I'd been an idiot all my life, that's why I was heading for a pauper's grave. So I have to make it clear to my family or somebody, when I die, if there isn't enough money, they can go, they get I think two weeks pension, and what I have, and they can, if that isn't enough, I can have a pauper's funeral. Oh dear, it's laughable really. (MacKinlay, 2001a, p. 194)

Even though Carol lives with multiple disabilities and other difficulties, she is still able to laugh at herself. Both Carol and the interviewer laughed a lot during the interview, and yet it seemed almost incongruent that she should seem so happy and so much at peace when speaking of the difficulties she was living with. This sense of joy within this frail older woman seemed to just bubble up from the core of her being, it was not surface emotion. This was an example of real transcendence, which is in turn a component of spiritual integrity in older people. This was not a denial of her difficulties, but a self-forgetting, and moving beyond the pain and suffering she experienced.

Carol seems to have a way of distancing herself from her difficulties, while not denying the truth of her situation. This is a real strength deep within herself. How did she learn to do this? Was it something within her personality? Was it learnt through education? Was it learnt through life experience? Did she deliberately set out to develop her wonderful sense of humour? I would suggest her humour is a great gift that benefits both herself and others she meets. It is strength in diversity, a strength that she needs to assist her to transcend the pain of fractured vertebrae, limited mobility, living alone, and the isolating and humiliating effects of incontinence.

Ann was another participant who laughed when remembering sad times, 'Oh I lost my brother, my younger brother with cancer' (about three years prior to the interview, Ann and her brother had been close to one another), and he was the youngest of the family. She said: 'We all found that very hard and I went to see him in hospital; (and he was), just like my father, praying out loud all over the ward' (both laugh). She paused and reflected, 'but I mean these things, you expect these things as you get older' She was struggling with the fact that it would not have been expected that her younger brother would have died before her.

In this example, both the informant and interviewer laughed together, at the mention of the informant's brother praying aloud in a hospital ward, while he was dying. This seems to be a case of cognitive dissonance. The situation was certainly not humorous, perhaps laughter served to lighten the moment, and both laughing together provided a way of being present to each other in a sensitive situation. Perhaps this too was a case of distancing from the death of her brother (MacKinlay, 2001a).

In a sense, these situations that I had written about in my book were hard for me to speak about in public, when I presented this paper at the conference *Spiritual Tasks of Ageing: Humour and Despair in Later Life*. I knew that I had protected the identities of all these people, but it seemed, when I thought of sharing these stories, that I was sharing intimate and very personal information. There is a sense of stepping on sacred ground. Maybe that is only the case for me, maybe not for you as readers. This is again a sign of being very close to others in sharing of things that verge on the unexplainable, things that were to some extent only able to be shared within a context of trust and humour.

What was the effect of laughter in these situations? In almost all examples, there was a raised consciousness of us both being in this situation together, a sharing of something very deep, and a privileged moment. The laughter was accompanied by smiling, quite often eye contact, and afterwards, a sense of release; certainly on my part, and, I suspect on the part of the informant.

Laughter in such circumstances is, I believe, an important way of connecting with the other person. It is a way of moving to another level of communication, and into the depths of the spiritual dimension. (Here I am using spiritual in a generic sense, perhaps more properly considered as soul, that is, the depth of one's being.) Humour and laughter can be used very effectively in a therapeutic situation. However, it is a strategy that cannot be forced. One cannot take a 'dose of laughter' although there are laughter groups now established in various places, apparently for that very purpose. Laughter used inappropriately would be disastrous to a relationship. It is only when a sense of trust exists between the parties that it is possible to use humour effectively.

It is often said that it takes a long time to develop trust between people. And yet, it must be remembered that in each case that I have discussed here, as researcher, I had only met the informant on one previous occasion. So it would appear that it is possible to develop communication to a deep level of connection and sharing in a relatively short period of time. I am suggesting it is possible to connect deeply, given that you have and use effective listening skills and exercise the ability of being sensitive to the needs of the person you are communicating with. This includes giving the speaker time to express themselves, to reflect on their thoughts and respond knowing that they will be listened to.

Were these examples of a spiritual nature? Yes, I believe so. It was a means of connecting with another human being in a deep way, in a situation that often was too deep for words. It was spontaneous, never contrived, I believe, by either of the parties. It was a way of 'being with' or 'being present' to one another. These are instances of self-transcendence.

HOW DOES A PERSON MOVE TO A PLACE WHERE THEY CAN USE HUMOUR TO SELF-TRANSCEND?

Although it is not my field, I understand that studies of biological responses to laughter do show chemical changes. It seems that humour and laughter can be a means of 'letting go' that is important, particularly in situations where we may feel we have no control over our circumstances. Humour and laughter can help us to move beyond, to arrive at a sense of the ridiculousness of a situation; to shift to a new perspective.

At times, possibly for most of us, life doesn't seem very funny. I remember some 40 years ago, as a nursing student, living in nurses' homes. Particularly when we worked on night duty, we would often come off duty in the morning, very tired and with issues of the previous night still on our minds. Over coffee a few of us would gather informally to talk about our 'night.' Often these discussions would end in laughter, as, in the light of day we could put a perspective on the experiences of the night. We were in a sense de-briefing. In another way, we were connecting deeply with each other, sharing, and in the process, we were transcending and distancing ourselves from our experiences. It was only then, that we were able to let go, and sleep during the day to be ready for another night of work.

There is a sense in which humour only works when the person is willing to be vulnerable and willing to respond to the story, the joke, or the laughter of others. Thus 'letting go' of anxieties and fears is a necessary pre-requisite to transcendence, in fact, it is part of transcendence, the person has to take a risk in allowing themselves to be open to humour. This risk-taking allows them to move towards transcendence.

DEATH, DYING AND LAUGHTER

I have already mentioned instances that revolved around death and humour. In a largely death-denying society, people are sometimes reluctant to speak of death. In fact some prefer not to name 'death' but rather speak of 'passing on' or 'passed away.' Indeed some recent literature has described studies where both staff and patients have used social discourse and humour to avoid discussion of impending death. Skilbeck (2003) suggests that in palliative care the form of light-hearted and humorous talk used by patients serves to allow the patients to distance themselves from their own deaths (p. 524).

The topic of death provided an instance of the use of humour for Eva (MacKinlay, 2001a). She fears being alone when she dies, and not being found. This woman shared how a friend of hers living alone, had died and had not been found for about a week. She joked about what might happen to her, she said: 'and she'd been dead a week. Now that shocked me and I thought (if I died alone). Oh and the two cats, you know they'd eat me.' In this instance Eva was sharing a very real fear of dying alone, but she laughed as she joked about the most unlikely and horrible outcome of dying alone. The possibility of dying alone did not disappear, but Eva seemed to find a way of expressing her fear and lifting her mood. This could be described as transcendence.

With the possible exception of Flora, who appeared to be seeking affirmation for her sharing, each of these informants appeared to be using laughter and humour as a way of connecting deeply when speaking of death and dying. In each case, there was a sense of the meaning of the conversation that transcended the mere words; body language was also a part of this, with smiling, eye contact and relaxed attitude. It would seem that laughter was used in a therapeutic manner in these examples.

However, the differences noticed between the females and males in the way that laughter was used (MacKinlay, 2001a) is also interesting, the women usually using humour to deepen the communication, while the men seemed at times to use humour to deflect from the sensitivity of the situation. This may be a factor of gender based differences in communication styles, or even a difference in expressing spirituality between the genders.

These instances of the use of humour link with the findings of Lefcourt and Martin (1986), who found that humour was related to matters of great 'profundity' of the human condition. In addition, McFadden (1990) suggested that humour was needed by older people to enable them to deal with some of the difficulties they encountered in life. The ability to laugh at themselves certainly was illustrated in the examples in this study. However, it is unclear whether the ability to laugh at oneself helps the individual to cope with a situation, or whether having to cope with difficult situations may help the individual to transcend the difficulties and in turn develop skills to be able to laugh at themselves.

HUMOUR EXPRESSED AMONGST PEOPLE LIVING WITH DEMENTIA

How do people with dementia use humour? The interviewer had only met this participant the day of this interview. During the interview the participant was asked: "do you have any fears right now?" The answer came straight back: "Yes, that I might die tomorrow, but nothing serious. I mean I can't do anything about it if it happens." Both the participant and interviewer laughed.

McFadden, Ingram, and Baldauf (2000) observed interactions between people with dementia and their use of humour. They found that there were many instances of naturally occurring humour in these interactions, and noted that in Frankl's terms, these people had mastered the "art of living," perhaps another way of saying they were transcending the situation.

All of the participants in the MacKinlay, Trevitt, and Hobart (2002) study have dementia. There were instances of sharp humour used in the interviews, humour that showed evidence of insight. In some instances during the small group sessions, the cognitively intact facilitator/staff member failed to see instances of humour used by these people who have dementia, and the humour was only apparent when the session transcripts were later transcribed and analysed.

Laughter was often present in the group sessions. In one instance a woman joked when she was asked about the hardest things in her life:

> My health I think, doing things I should do, like clean my teeth. I mean everybody says have you cleaned your teeth before you get into bed, yes I've cleaned them tonight, and my Annie will say, my goodness me then you don't have to get out of bed again then and clean them, making a joke of it, because I always forget my teeth at night.

The following interchange reflects the sense of fun that some of these people retain and their interaction within the group. The facilitator asked where she could assist them in finding meaning now, resulting in this exchange:

Dorothy: "I find things to interest myself, I read a lot, do exercises, I run up and down my room a hundred times."
Facilitator: "She does, she runs everywhere Bob."
Bob responds: "She's probably got the foundations improved in her home."
Dorothy: "I don't feel my age, until I look in the mirror."
Bob: "You look pretty good too."
Dorothy: "Oh thanks dear and you always look lovely."
Bob: "Thank you."

This is part of a transcribed conversation between nursing home residents who have dementia. It has been apparent in these studies (MacKinlay et al., 2002-04) that being able to communicate in a supported and affirmed way is highly beneficial for these vulnerable nursing home residents. In a pilot study completed in 2002 (MacKinlay, Trevitt and Hobart, 2002) of people living with dementia, humour could be seen as a means of transcending many of the hard parts of life. It is noted that humour was used spontaneously on a number of occasions. These instances were initiated by group members and led to increased interaction in the group.

CONCLUSION

Humour was seen to be used frequently among older people in these studies, including independent living, those in residential care and those living with dementia in residential care. It seemed that Frankl's concept of self forgetting was active within these interchanges, of older people telling their stories, and of people who were living with dementia supporting each other and laughing about memory loss. The spiritual task and process of ageing involving transcendence can be expressed as a dying to self. Where this occurs, the person is able to move beyond their difficulties and more effectively deal with the issues of living in the present. Humour appears to play an important function in this process.

In this paper, the spiritual task of transcendence has been linked to humour. It is possible that humour may be used therapeutically, in pastoral care and other areas of aged care. Humour may be both a means and an outcome of spiritual integrity. Humour is more than just jokes, it can assist people to transcend disabilities and losses, to face death and to connect with others.

NOTE

1. MacKinlay, Trevitt, and Hobart, 2002.

REFERENCES

Erikson, E. H., Erikson, J. M., & Kivnick, H. Q. (1986) *Vital Involvement in Old Age.* New York: W. W. Norton & Co.
Frankl, V. E. (1986) *The Doctor and the Soul.* New York: Vintage Books.
Frankl, V. E. (1997) *Man's Search for Ultimate Meaning.* New York: Plenum Press.
Frankl, V. E. (1984) *Man's Search for Meaning.* New York: Washington Square Press.
Lefcourt, H. M., & Martin, R. A. (1986) *Humor and Life Stress: Antidote to Adversity.* New York: Springer-Verlag.
McFadden, S. H. (1990) 'Authentic Humor as an Expression of Spiritual Maturity.' In Seeber, J. J., *Spiritual Maturity in the Later Years.* New York: The Haworth Press, Inc.
McFadden, S. H., Ingram, M., & Baldauf, C. (2000) Actions, feelings, and values: Foundations of meaning and personhood in dementia. *Journal of Religious Gerontology,* 11(3/4), 67-86.
MacKinlay, E. B. (1998) The Spiritual Dimension of ageing: Meaning in Life, Response to *Meaning and Well Being in Ageing.* Unpublished doctoral thesis. Melbourne: La Trobe University.
MacKinlay, E. B. (2001a) *The Spiritual Dimension of Ageing.* London: Jessica Kingsley Publishers.
MacKinlay, E.B. (2001b) Health, healing, and wholeness in frail elderly people. *Journal of Religious Gerontology.* 13, 2, 25-34.

MacKinlay, Trevitt, & Hobart (2002) *The Search for Meaning: Quality of life for the person with dementia.* University of Canberra Collaborative Grant Report (Unpublished).

Skilbeck, J., & Payne, S. (2003) Emotional support and the role if the Clinical Nurse Specialists in palliative care. *Journal of Advanced Nursing.* 43. 5, 521-530.

Wilcock, P. (2004) The Caged Bird: Thoughts on the challenge of living with stroke. In A. Jewell, *Ageing, Spirituality, and Well-Being.* London: Jessica Kingsley Publishers.

Dementia, Identity, and Spirituality

John Killick

SUMMARY. A key question asked about dementia is whether it destroys identity. There is a weighty body of opinion and attitude against the preservation of selfhood in the condition. In recent years, however, the contrary view has increasingly been put. A significant element in the strategies proposed by adherents of the latter stance is the influence on the development of dementia of the attitudes and practices of caregivers. The theory is put forward that the capacity to embrace change in those surrounding the person is crucial to the maintenance of wellbeing. The author goes on to argue that a decline in cognitive capacity may lead to a growth in spiritual powers, which poses a challenge to us all. *[Article copies available for a fee from The Haworth Document Delivery Service: 1-800-HAWORTH. E-mail address: <docdelivery@haworthpress. com> Website: <http://www.HaworthPress.com> © 2004 by The Haworth Press, Inc. All rights reserved.]*

KEYWORDS. Dementia, identity, change, wellbeing, expression, spirituality

John Killick was for many years a teacher and is now a freelance writer, lecturer, and researcher based in Yorkshire, England. He is part-time Associate Research Fellow in Communication Through the Arts at Dementia Services Development Centre, University of Stirling. He is co-author with Kate Allan of *Communication and the Care of People with Dementia* and his collections of poems have been published in book and CD form by the *Journal of Dementia Care*.

[Haworth co-indexing entry note]: "Dementia, Identity, and Spirituality." Killick, John. Co-published simultaneously in *Journal of Religious Gerontology* (The Haworth Pastoral Press, an imprint of The Haworth Press, Inc.) Vol. 16, No. 3/4, 2004, pp. 59-74; and: *Spirituality of Later Life: On Humor and Despair* (ed: Rev. Elizabeth MacKinlay) The Haworth Pastoral Press, an imprint of The Haworth Press, Inc., 2004, pp. 59-74. Single or multiple copies of this article are available for a fee from The Haworth Document Delivery Service [1-800-HAWORTH, 9:00 a.m. - 5:00 p.m. (EST). E-mail address: docdelivery@haworthpress.com].

http://www.haworthpress.com/web/JRG
© 2004 by The Haworth Press, Inc. All rights reserved.
Digital Object Identifier: 10.1300/J078v16n03_05

PART ONE: DEMENTIA AND IDENTITY

'Does dementia destroy the self?' is one of the central questions asked about the condition, and cannot be answered categorically. It has been the subject of articles, papers, even whole books, and is likely to occasion more. Amongst the most recent to address it at least in part are Thomas DeBaggio's *Losing My Mind: An Intimate Look at Life with Alzheimer's* (DeBaggio, 2003) and Steven R. Sabat's *The Experience of Alzheimer's: Life Through a Tangled Veil* (Sabat, 2001).

The perception that with the onset of the condition the person gradually disappears seems to be one shared by many carers, some people with dementia, and a number of doctors, psychologists and psychiatrists, particularly those wedded to the medical model. Here is the psychogeriatrician Alan Jacques writing in 1992 (this text was republished unchanged in 2000):

> At the final stages the patient may be assumed to have no real subjective awareness; no sense of self at all, and to be in this sense mentally 'dead.' (Jacques, 1992, 172)

A recent issue of the Newsletter *Dementia in Scotland* published by Alzheimer Scotland/Action on Dementia' carried an article by a carer under the title 'The Long Goodbye.' Anyone familiar with such publications would recognise the assertions it contains. The first paragraph reads:

> My husband died a few months ago. He had been suffering from dementia and I had said goodbye to the real person long before his physical presence left us. (Porter, 2002, 7)

Thomas DeBaggio, writing as a man diagnosed with dementia, says:

> On a pleasant sunny day like this several years from now, I will die with no sense of what is happening and surrounded by mourners who can know nothing of my inner turmoil, a pain I will never be able to utter in my Alzheimer silence. (DeBaggio, 2003, 174)

In his case, however, he seems more to be expressing apprehensiveness, the fear of what might happen as a result of his loss of memory, rather than a reaction to its actual occurrence.

Alzheimer's Associations are also prone to asserting worst case scenarios. In 2002 Alzheimer Scotland/Action on Dementia mounted its most expensive advertising campaign to date under the by-line 'Are You Losing the Person You Knew?'[1] with the words gradually fading from left to right, and the 'i' in the word 'losing' lower-case in the midst of capitals, the clear intention being to emphasise the loss of identity involved in the dementia process. Here, I suggest, the motivation is more cynical than truth-telling, as many charities seem to swell their coffers by presenting the most pessimistic viewpoint, seemingly unaware that by so doing they are 'selling short' the very people whom they claim to represent.[2]

It can be seen from the above examples that there is a weighty body of theory and attitude against the maintaining of selfhood in dementia. Those who hold the converse opinion often seem to have an uphill struggle. Yet a dispassionate examination of the evidence would suggest that logic may well be on their side. Let us examine the nature of identity and the ways in which, in dementia, the individual may be put under siege.

Identity is fundamentally experienced by the human being by the use of the terms 'I' and 'me' amongst other speech conventions, and through various non-verbal observations of, and gesturing towards, the body in self-acknowledgement. It is through a whole series of such manifestations, from moment to moment, day to day and year to year, that the individual perceives a continuity and consistency of performance which can be designated 'the self.' It relies upon interactions with the environment and with others, and the concepts of past, present and future times, to reinforce this concept of wholeness. Memory must play a key role in this process, and any lapses will result in problems for the maintenance of unity of self-consciousness. It is precisely because dementia often results in memory loss that the chain can be broken, and life experience, and thus a sense of identity, may be fractured, leading to confusion and loss of confidence.

Michael Ignatieff (1994), in his novel *Scar Tissue* has his main character reflect upon the dementia of his mother in the following terms:

> I suspected that the breakdown in her memory was a symptom of larger disruption in her ability to create and sustain a coherent image of herself over time. It dawned on me that her condition offered me an unrepeatable opportunity to observe the relation between selfhood and memory. . . . My mistake had been to suppose that a memory image could subsist apart from the self, that memories could persist apart from the act of speaking or thinking about them from a given standpoint. It was just this junction between past and present that she was losing. She was wondering who the 'I' was in her own sentences. Nevertheless the son goes on

to assert that in other ways his mother displays a reassuring consistency: In spite of all this, her gestures, her smile, her voice remained unchanged. A blurred vision of her charm survived, together with hints of her sense of Humour. She was suffering from a disturbance of her soul, not just a loss of memory, yet she was still intact. (Ignatieff, 1994, 53)

In an article in which he is able to make first person assertions about a condition which is hereditary in his family, Ignatieff speaks of 'the primary self,' which he defines as follows:

In the people I have known who have succumbed to the disease, there still remains, at the end, a primary and incorrigible core of selfhood. That essential self remains in their expression, their gait, some tiny habit, some gesture, some faint glint of Humour, even a liking for ice cream. (Ignatieff, 1992, 4.7)

It is interesting to compare this account with that of another perceptive commentator, Oliver Sacks, the neurologist:

In dementias, one may find all sorts of specific losses. . . . and, as the disease worsens, a reduction of personal identity. And yet this reduction is virtually never complete; it is as if identity has such a robust, widespread neural basis; as if personal style is so deeply ingrained in the nervous system that it is never wholly lost, at least while there is still any mental life present at all. (Sacks, 1998)

Sabat, in the book already mentioned, mounts a sustained attack on the identity-loss position. In a series of detailed case studies he shows how the characteristics of each individual remain, and suggests ways in which memory and confidence can be enhanced. The main drawback of his argument, and it is a serious one, is that each of his subjects was a high-achieving academic, still comparatively early in the development of their dementias, and with a sense of self which is probably unusually well developed.

In a remarkable article, Morris Friedell, a man diagnosed with Alzheimer's five years previously, demonstrates how he has increased his cognitive functioning by following a 10-point program of his own devising. He is remarkably positive in his approach. Speaking of someone in his position he says:

He is faced with a challenge analogous to the adolescent's-of creating his own self rather than being largely a product of his biology and environment, but much more difficult. Hopefully, the person with dementia faces the challenge with the belief that the essence of his selfhood has not been truly diminished by the deficits and losses. (Friedell, 2003, 82)

Again, with Friedell, another ex-academic, there is no doubt that he is blessed with determination, intellectual capacity, and self-possession well above the norm.

Where Sabat makes his most valuable contribution to the debate is in the emphasis that he places on the influence on the development of their dementia of family, friends, and colleagues surrounding the person. He makes clear that this can be of a positive or a negative nature, and that too often it is of the latter kind. If his subjects, with all their inner resources, are beset by misunderstandings and rejections which pose a challenge to their personhood, then how much more devastating must those challenges be to individuals, the vast majority in any population, whose grasp of their own selfhood is more fragile? Sabat fails to acknowledge the wider implications of his insights here, except by implication.

We are entering the territory of the apologists for the psychosocial approach to dementia. This maintains that neurological impairment is only one aspect of the condition, and that it is how others without dementia view the person which contributes significantly to the development of symptoms. The concepts of wellbeing and illbeing are useful here, and so is that of insight. If those around the person lack insight in their dealings with them, then this may create serious consequences for that person's confidence and self-esteem. Withdrawal into the self may occur, and communication with others lessened as a protective measure or in frustration at failures to connect. Relations, friends, and staff may then abandon attempts at understanding under the mistaken belief that such efforts are fruitless. Kitwood, this movement's most passionate apologist, identifies some of these 'put-downs' as 'personal detractors' as part of a wider 'malignant social psychology' (Kitwood, 1997) and demonstrates how a state of illbeing can easily, if unintentionally, be created by those entrusted with a person's welfare.

At the same time Kitwood outlines the conditions necessary for the restoration of wellbeing (which in the most dramatic cases he calls 'rementia'):

It is often the case that a dementia sufferer who is visibly withdrawing or becoming demoralised, is transformed by a little real attention and human contact. It is as if he or she needs to be re-called to the world of persons, where a place is no longer guaranteed. At such times one or more of the indicators of wellbeing may be shown, only to fade quickly. Wellbeing, then, for dementia sufferers, often appears to be fragile or short-lived. Whereas some individuals with the full range of cognitive powers have 'inner' reserves to draw on, or at least well-developed capacities for carrying on in a 'frozen' state, those who are some way into a dementing illness do not. Often they seem to have virtually no reserves, and to be drifting towards the threshold of unbeing. Their personhood needs to be continually replenished, their selfhood continually evoked and reassured. (Kitwood, 1992, 285)

What would this kind of all-embracing project be like in practice? I am not aware of any in-depth accounts of individual attempts to arrest the development of the condition in those whose confusion is severe.

There is, however, an excellent research report focusing on the minutiae of positive care strategies in a residential setting: Anne Vittoria spent a year observing Starrmount Alzheimer's Special Care Unit in America, and her findings are so encouraging that they need to be recounted in some detail.

Vittoria found what she defines as 'communicative care,' where the task was perceived as 'to *assume* there are surviving selves in the Alzheimer's residents and endeavour to preserve, protect, support, and engage these selves as *the* essential part of the work' (Vittoria, 1998) (author's italics, p. 92). Vittoria herself expresses the philosophy in the following words 'Caregiving. . . . is not something done *to* but primarily done *with* the resident, a caring for, instead of an abstract caring about' (author's italics, p. 104). A charge nurse puts it like this:

The most important thing is for the resident to keep their individual self, the quality of their being. You know, a lot of times people think that because they're like that, they don't have a quality of life. But they do, because you'd be surprised some of the things that come up. Because we bring it out of them. (Vittoria, 1998, 105)

Clumsy though the phrasing may be here, it is clear that the essential ethic of the unit has been absorbed. In the course of her paper Vittoria analyses the staff's successes by means of a number of helpful concepts:

- 'felt meaning' is non-cognitive understanding developed between residents and staff.
- 'destinations of the mind' are the geographical and emotional places individual residents occupy.
- 'traits of being' are surviving characteristics which the staff are able to bring out (often to the amazement of family and visitors).
- 'initiating' is the process of entering into negotiation with a resident in a state of mindfulness of the possibilities.
- 'nurturing' is building on what has been achieved in a spirit of celebration; it 'involves supporting the *response* to life of a persisting self and recognizing a continuing *capacity for creating meaning* from those under one's care' (author's italics, Vittoria, 1998, 128).

Vittoria distinguishes between what she calls 'the series of selves.' These consist of 'the storied self' made up of the memories a resident carries, 'the new self' which exists in the now, and 'the imagined self' which staff hold of each resident as they speculate about their past lives.

A key point is the distinction between the functional aspects of the condition and the self as an individual:

> The central thrust of the staff is striving for a distinct separation of the person and "the disease." . . . When attribution to the disease is used by staff, it appears to be used not as a way of labelling but of *preserving the self free of a label*; just the opposite of what we ordinarily think of attribution resulting in: a label, a stigmatized status. While the disease is referenced, it is generally referenced as a *defence* for the acting person. (author's italics, p. 124)

Vittoria does not claim that every interaction between staff and resident at Starrmount is a success. Where it is perceived as inadequate, and illbeing results, she analyses it. One of the failures she pinpoints is where 'the voice of the lifeworld' meets 'the voice of medicine,' in other words the psychosocial and the clinical come into conflict.

It is rare for institutional provision to be subjected to such insightful examination, and we need more reports of this nature. We also need more studies of individuals at various stages of the condition and in different social settings, so that we may see if there are common factors of caring which can be applied, to enhance the communication skills and personhood of those with the diagnosis. We also need to move to a situation where every individual with dementia is afforded the kind of enlightened consideration Sabat gives to his clients, and this entails drastic attitude-change on the part of providers, as well as having major resource implications.

PART TWO: DEMENTIA AND SPIRITUALITY

How we live our lives is necessarily a compromise between the instinctive and the learned, and the place we occupy on the spectrum will differ from person to person, according to the nature of our upbringing, temperament and experience among other factors. It is probably most clearly exemplified in our reactions to the unexpected-those occasions when we are thrown up against events to which we have little choice but to react. At one extreme some people will reach for the explanation nearest to hand, something which has served themselves and others well in the past, and could be reasonably relied upon to do so again. For some of these individuals organised religion can provide the prop, for others a perceived solidarity emanating from the family, or a social group. Either way thought does not necessarily play a significant part, it is more a matter of a learned habitual reaction.

At the other extreme come those who take a more sceptical stance. They are not satisfied with what is presented to them, but are prepared to exist in a state of suspension, while they ask questions and actively seek their own solutions. For these people a prolonged period of self-doubt may ensue, they are ready to endure pain rather than rush into the arms of the nearest available consoling philosophy. Those who take the latter course are likely to be in a minority, since it calls for particular reserves of determination and resilience to sustain the quest. The inner conflict they may experience has been well expressed in her poem 'Answers' by Elizabeth Jennings:

> . . . the big answers clamoured to be moved
> into my life. Their great audacity
> shouted to be acknowledged and believed.
>
> Even when all small answers build up to
> protection of my spirit, still I hear
> big answers striving for their overthrow
>
> And all the great conclusions coming near. (Jennings, 1986, 26/7)

When dementia strikes, how does the individual whose responses are already allied to one or other of these approaches cope? This is one of those questions it is easier to pose than to answer. It requires us to have a full knowledge of the person prior to diagnosis, and this is something which professionals in the field do not often possess. Family carers who are able to call upon history of the person allied to insight may be in a better position to answer. Here, by way of example, is Susan Miller, a novelist, who in her book *The Story of My Father* subjects her clergyman parent's extraordinary embrace of Alzheimer's to the following analysis:

> . . . in general, his acceptance of his illness-an illness that would take his intellect, his connection with other people, his ability to speak, to eat, to walk, to reason-seemed to speak of the inner resources he had because he was God's, as he saw it. He thought of this illness without ego, precisely *without* the sense of self and grief for the loss of self that would afflict me if I found I had Alzheimer's disease. In this way, the way in which I am very much 'my own' for better or worse, my father was not. This was the source for him of an almost unfathomable strength as he began his slow decline. And this was part, too, of who he was. (Miller, 2003, 169)

One of the first first-person accounts of dementia to appear was that of Robert Davis in America, and he was a clergyman. His account of the crisis in his life precipitated by the onset of confusion followed by the diagnosis, *My Journey Into Alzheimer's Disease*, is both moving and illuminating. Here was a man of steadfast conviction filled with a proselytising zeal. His reaction was much more dramatic than that of Sue Miller's father-panic and despair set in. And then:

> One night in Wyoming as I lay in a motel crying out to my Lord, my long desperate prayers were suddenly answered. As I lay there in the blackness silently shrieking out my often repeated prayer, there was suddenly a light that seemed to fill my very soul. The sweet, holy presence of Christ came to me. He spoke to my spirit and said 'Take my peace. Stop your struggling. It is all right. This is all in keeping with my will for your life. I now release you from the burden of the heavy yoke of pastoring that I placed upon you. Relax and stop struggling in your desperate search for answers. I will hold you. Lie back in your Shepherd's arms, and take my peace.' (Davis, 1989, 62)

On reflection he summarises this experience in the following words:

Many Christians have found that when life completely tumbles in, when they are without strength or any hope or help for themselves, or when their minds become too tangled to even hold thoughts, that God overrules the circumstances and that Christ comes to minister to them at the very point of their need. (Davis, 1989, 67)

And:

My new and simple service to him was to rest in him and moment by moment take his peace and use his strength to simply live . . . From now on, my lot in life would be to be specially held by the Shepherd, letting him fully care for me. (Davis, 1989, 63)

It is as if the certainties which had surrounded and bolstered up Davis had suddenly been removed and he was floundering temporarily without any means of support. Then came the realisation that the faith was still there but manifesting itself in different ways, and required him to make an adjustment in his lifestyle to accommodate it. Instead of being one who dispenses reassurance he had to become one who accepted it. From being a man who functioned in one way he was given a bitter taste of how it might be to be required to function without his faith; fortunately for him he found a way to accept the embrace of his religion once more.

David Shenk is a journalist, and in *The Forgetting* he has written a very fair-minded book on dementia, balancing the technical and the experiential in his search for the meaning of the condition. At one point he writes:

While medical science gives us many tools for staying alive it cannot help us with the art of living or dying. Life, in its precious transience, is something we can only define on our own terms. With Alzheimer's disease the caregiver's challenge is to escape the medical confines of disease and to assemble a new humanity in this loss. (Shenk D., 2001)

Dementia, of course, poses the same challenge to the caregiver as to the person with the condition-how to adjust to the unexpected and bewildering changes that may occur in that person. Shenk is quite right to identify this further challenge to the family member, though-that of accommodating fundamental modifications in the functioning of the loved one whilst themselves remaining comparatively unchanged. In the broadest sense this will almost inevitably involve an adjustment in dependence. Many caregivers speak of this in terms of role reversal, for example, gradually the adult mother or father becomes as a child and the son or daughter takes on the responsibilities of a parent. In a marriage, what had previously existed as a relationship based on equality can become destabilised, and one where stresses had already been manifest may find the fault-lines develop into fissures. The particular modes of operation of families can find themselves tested to the limit. The Alzheimer Societies' Newsletters are full of despairing cries from anxious and wellmeaning relatives unable to understand or adapt to rapidly changing circumstances. This may be where the more open and flexible caregiver is more successful in providing the kind of responses the situation demands.

Sunny Vogler in her book *Dementia: The Loss . . . the Love . . . the Laughter* seems to be just such a person. She describes her attitude in the following words:

> My friends and family were continually amazed at my desire and ability to change my life at the drop of a hat. Deliberating over a new idea required only a short time to weigh the pros and cons before making a decision. When I was asked 'How do you do it?' I answered, 'First of all, I love taking the risk, for me security is boring.' (Vogler, 2003, 25)

She decides to devote her life full-time to her mother and meet all the vicissitudes spontaneously and comprehensively. She rejects the help offered by medical staff, social workers, even that of Alzheimer's Care Groups which she sees operating as shoulders to cry on, not as networks to inspire to greater efforts:

> The initial impression I derived from listening to their stories and complaints was that spouses have a much harder time accepting their loved one's illness. The changes they see occurring are fought against and strongly denied for as long as possible; very often by both parties. (Vogler, 2003, 65)

Vogler does not fight or deny, and encourages her mother to do likewise, despite the fact that she had suffered much at her mother's hands throughout her childhood, and that this had been succeeded by many years of estrangement. The result is that she is able to write passages like the following:

Mother was different, and discovering who she was each day was a delight. The bitterness she had lived with was draining from her mind . . . and in its place was a new pleasant outlook that seemed to surprise and please both of us. More than once she gave me a loving look and simply whispered 'thank you.' These were the rewards I had missed in my childhood and were so welcome now. (Vogler, 2003, 37)

Vogler supplies a remarkable role-model for those in intimate relationships with people with dementia. An example of where awareness of what is happening can be allied to inflexibility of attitude is supplied by Thomas De Baggio (whose book *Losing My Mind* has already been quoted from). Although he is still active, and can speak and write with impressive coherence, he can find little satisfaction in this and few consolations that can stem from his diagnosis. He is obsessed by what the future may bring, and what he characterises as an inevitable and inexorable decline into confusion:

I live a new life of slow motion, stumbling with lost confidence. New things are torturous, confusing, and hard to understand. Even the old stuff of my life is not always familiar but with time and patience it is often recognizable. My eyes tear for no reason and I explode, when in better times I might have laughed. Send me away. I cannot stand to live in this dying body with its floating alphabet. I do not want to see the life of my future. (De Baggio, 2002)

A woman whom I encountered in a nursing home provides a more complex example of becoming reconciled to the changes which have occurred. She was sitting in the far corner of a lounge singing quietly to herself. The sound was even and mellifluous. The staff assured me that she was of a contented disposition, and that her continuous singing was a sign of her happiness with her situation. When I moved closer to her I was able to hear and write down the words she sang, which were obviously improvised:

I don't know what to do
I want to go home
I can sit here but
I don't seem happy any more
I don't know what to do
I want to but

I can't any more
I want to lay
I don't know when it'll be
I want it so let me have it
Don't make it so hard for me
O World, I don't know what to do
I want to see my sunset
I want it as it was promised
I'm waiting for the hour
I want to see my sunset good. (Benson & Killick, 2002)

    (Printed with permission.)

To speak in terms of happiness or sadness here seems inappropriate. There is much ambiguity in the woman's words. She wants to go 'home,' she wants to 'lay,' she's 'waiting for the hour': it is difficult to see these as other than references to the end of her life. And she appears caught between the worlds of life and death, with an inability to act in such a way as to resolve the issue. At the outset she states her dilemma, and she repeats this statement later, but by prefixing it with the words 'O World' she turns it into an appeal for help. The lines:

    I want to see my sunset
    I want it as it was promised

seem like a reference to religion and the possible rewards of an after-life. And the word 'good' added to the first of these lines to form the last line of the song adds fervour to the prayer which is being uttered. Why does this woman sing her poem rather than speak it? Probably because of the pressure of feeling behind such sentiments, and song is the natural language of the emotions.

This leads me to a key observation in considering the strategies people with dementia may develop in order to cope with the changes which are occurring in and around them. Although these changes undoubtedly involve cognitive abilities, and although there may be commensurate emotional reactions to such changes, there is no evidence to show that people lose the capacity to feel per se in the way they lose the capacity to reason. That is why it is so important that individuals be given opportunities to express themselves, verbally and non-verbally, especially the latter in instances where spoken and written language abilities fall away. The arts have a special part to play in this process of opening up pathways for the person which may hitherto have been closed or remained relatively unexplored.

But alongside these positive developments, which can only surely be accomplished by and through individuals possessed of exploratory mind-sets, there needs to be created a culture of appreciation and encouragement. It is no good offering people with dementia new approaches if we are not prepared to celebrate their achievements. Here is where our overvaluing of intellectual prowess comes in, and provides such a disservice to those who, for whatever reason, lack or are losing skills in this area. As Morris Friedell, himself someone forced to wear the dementia label, writes:

> In our contemporary 'hypercognitive' society, to be afflicted with a dementing disease is to be reborn as an 'untouchable' member of an inferior caste. (Friedell, 2003)

Is it possible that the very deprivation of cognitive capacity can in some people with dementia lead to the growth of spiritual powers? This is a question which, for the present, remains a rhetorical one. But it is surely true that dementia provides those of us without the condition with a special challenge: that of valuing the person for their essence rather than for the social, economic or political accretions which our complex civilization has built up and which tend to obscure the basic human values of honest reaction, of spontaneous truthfulness. Maybe people with dementia are themselves leading the way in identifying this fundamental quality for us? Christine Boden and Barb Noon pose it in my final quotations:

> The unique essence of 'me' is at my core, and this is what will remain with me to the end. I will be perhaps more truly 'me' than I have ever been. (Boden, 1997)

Burning Bright

Sometimes I picture myself
like a candle.
I used to be a candle about eight feet tall-
burning bright.
Now, every day I lose
a little bit of me.

Someday the candle will be
very small.
But the flame will be
just as bright. (Noon, 2003)

(Printed with permission.)

NOTES

1. *Dementia in Scotland Newsletter*, Issue 34, p. 1.
2. It is significant that this publicity drive elicited a response from a group of carers in a subsequent issue of the Society's Newsletter which included the following: 'We felt that the campaign this year was extremely negative and did much to damage the positive image of people with dementia that had been built up over recent years.' (*Dementia in Scotland,* Issue 40, December 2002, p. 12).

REFERENCES

Benson, S., & Killick J. (2002). *Creativity in Dementia Care Calendar 2003.* London: Hawker.

Boden, C. (1997). *Who Will I Be When I Die?* London: Harper Collins. 49/50.

Davis, R. (1989). *My Journey Into Alzheimer's Disease.* Illinois: Tyndale House. 62.

De Baggio, T. (2002). *Losing My Mind: An Intimate Look at Life with Alzheimer's.* New York: The Free Press.

DeBaggio, T. (2003). *Losing My Mind: An Intimate Look at Life with Alzheimer's.* New York: The Free Press.

Dementia in Scotland Newsletter, Issue 34, 1.

Friedell, M. (2003). Dementia Survival: A New Vision. *Alzheimer's Care Quarterly,* 4, 2, 79-84, 82.

Friedell, M. (2003). Dementia Survival: A New Vision. *Alzheimer's Care Quarterly,* April/June, 79-84.

Ignatieff, M. (1992). *A taste of ice cream is all you know.* The Observer 4.7.

Ignatieff, M. (1994). *Scar Tissue.* London: Vintage. 53.

Jacques, A. (1992). *Understanding Dementia.* Edinburgh: Churchill Livingstone, 172.

Jennings, E. (1986). *Collected Poems.* Manchester: Carcanet, 26/7.

Kitwood T. (1992). Towards a Theory of Dementia Care: Personhood and Wellbeing. *Ageing and Society,* 12, 269-287 285.

Kitwood, T. (1997). *Dementia Reconsidered.* Buckingham: Open University Press. 45-9.

Miller, S. (2003). *The Story of My Father.* New York: Alfred A. Knopf. 169.

Noon, B. (2003). In Benson S., & Killick J. *Creativity in Dementia Care Calendar 2004.* Hawker: London.

Porter, H. (2002). The Long Goodbye. *Dementia in Scotland Newsletter.* Issue 38 7.

Sabat, S.R. (2001). *The Experience of Alzheimer's: Life Through a Tangled Veil.* Oxford: Blackwells.

Sacks, O. (1998). *Music and the Brain.* In Tomaino C. (Ed.), *Classical Applications of Music in Neurologic Brain Rehabilitation.* (1-18). St. Louis: MMB Music.

Shenk, D. (2001). *The Forgetting.* New York: Doubleday.

Vittoria, A.K. (1998). Preserving Selves: Identity Work and Dementia. *Research on Aging*, 20, 1, 91-136.

Vogler, S. (2003). *Dementia: The Loss. . . . the Love . . . . the Laughter.* USA: 1st Books Library 25.

Ways of Studying Religion, Spirituality, and Aging: The Social Scientific Approach

Elizabeth MacKinlay, PhD, RN
Susan H. McFadden, PhD

SUMMARY. This paper presents an overview of methods of research most commonly used in research in the field of aging, religion and spirituality. It discusses the reasons for doing research and the applicability of findings to practice, providing a guide to practitioners in becoming discerning consumers of research in this field. The paper also provides examples of research in this field, using both quantitative and qualitative methods. *[Article copies available for a fee from The Haworth Document Delivery Service: 1-800-HAWORTH. E-mail address: <docdelivery@haworthpress.com> Website: <http://www.HaworthPress.com> © 2004 by The Haworth Press, Inc. All rights reserved.]*

Elizabeth MacKinlay is Director, Centre for Ageing and Pastoral Studies, School of Theology, Charles Sturt University, 15 Blackall Street, Barton, ACT Australia 2600 (E-mail: emackinlay@csu.edu.au). Susan H. McFadden is affiliated with the Department of Psychology, University of Wisconsin Oshkosh, Oshkosh, WI 54901 USA (E-mail: mcfadden@uwosh.edu).

The project: *The Search for Meaning: Quality of life for the person with dementia* was made possible through a University of Canberra Collaborative Research Grant with research industry partners Anglican Retirement Community Services and Wesley Gardens Aged Care, 2000-01.

[Haworth co-indexing entry note]: "Ways of Studying Religion, Spirituality, and Aging: The Social Scientific Approach." MacKinlay, Elizabeth, and Susan H. McFadden. Co-published simultaneously in *Journal of Religious Gerontology* (The Haworth Pastoral Press, an imprint of The Haworth Press, Inc.) Vol. 16, No. 3/4, 2004, pp. 75-90; and: *Spirituality of Later Life: On Humor and Despair* (ed: Rev. Elizabeth MacKinlay) The Haworth Pastoral Press, an imprint of The Haworth Press, Inc., 2004, pp. 75-90. Single or multiple copies of this article are available for a fee from The Haworth Document Delivery Service [1-800-HAWORTH, 9:00 a.m. - 5:00 p.m. (EST). E-mail address: docdelivery@haworthpress.com].

KEYWORDS. Religion, spirituality, aging, research design, grounded theory

WHY SHOULD PEOPLE WHO CARE ABOUT RELIGION, SPIRITUALITY, AND AGING UNDERSTAND RESEARCH DESIGN?

People who work in practice settings with older people may sometimes wonder about the need for doing research. A lot of research is now being conducted and reported in both professional journals and the popular media, and it is important that practitioners understand the research findings being reported. A basic and important question is, will this research make a difference to my practice and to the well being of those I care for? Much of what is reported in the media comes without any detail of how the research was conducted and sometimes the claims of research made in the media are exaggerated. Those who work with older people need to know how to assess this research and to know whether what is being reported has any validity or not; it is vitally important for all professionals who work with older adults to be intelligent consumers of research. To do this, it is necessary to know how research is conducted.

Two other reasons can be put forward to justify the need to know about research. Practitioners need to be able to assess the findings of research to know whether it should inform and/or form the basis for changed practice. Also, awareness of the complexity of conducting research and reaching conclusions is needed. Knowing the basics of the research process provides an understanding of what is involved in doing research and producing outcomes. Researchers need to collaborate with practitioners in their applied settings in order to conduct many types of research. Those practitioners need to be knowledgeable so they can assess the research plans to see if they are ethical, feasible, and worthwhile, given the investment of time and resources that are usually required of the cooperating facility.

Why Do We Do Research?

In terms of the context for this article, research is done so we can draw valid, reliable conclusions about, in the context of this article, older people, their health and well-being, religious practices and beliefs and spirituality, and the relationships among these variables. This is important when we are trying to meet accreditation guidelines and best practice standards, that is, to inform evidence-based practice. Research provides information on which to base care standards. It is only through good research that it can be known what works, what does not, and why.

Who Will We Study?

Researchers always face the problem of finding a representative sample as it is all too easy to study a sample that is biased in some way. It is important to take into account the variables of race, ethnicity, class, and gender that are intricately connected to religious and spiritual practices. When studying the spiritual dimension and religion, it is also important to take denominational differences into account. Too often in the past, religion has been treated generically, ignoring differences between and within denominations. This is true of all religions, as there is a breadth of variation within each.

What Kind of Data Will We Collect?

This question has to be asked before starting every research project. There are a variety of sources of data. The most common sources are: interviews (structured and open-ended), questionnaires/surveys, diaries, structured observations, and experiments.

What Are Some Basic Approaches to Doing Research Used by Social Scientists Who Study Religion, Spirituality, and Aging?

As in other disciplines of study and practice, a range of approaches are used, depending on a number of factors including the type of questions being asked in the project and the characteristics of the people being studied. It is important to choose methods of study that will provide the best data for the particular project. The conclusions drawn are often very much a function of the study designs chosen.

The two main types of research methodology-qualitative and quantitative-differ from each other greatly (see Reker, 1995, for a detailed discussion of these methods, McFadden, Brennan, & Patrick, 2000 for examples of studies). Qualitative research is less structured, and often uses interviews or case studies of one person. Typically, qualitative research does not employ large numbers of participants, nor does it use statistical methods for data analysis. Quantitative research, on the other hand, traditionally uses random or stratified samples of participants assigned to experimental and control treatments. Quantitative research also employs surveys and questionnaires, with the data submitted to statistical analyses. Quantitative research investigates relationships among or differences between variables under investigation. Both methodologies have important uses in research in ageing, religion, and spirituality. A brief review of both types will be given as they are applied in work with older adults.

A. *Qualitative Research*

Qualitative methods of research are valuable in exploring new areas that have been little studied previously. When questionnaires are constructed, there is always the danger that the person constructing the questionnaire may not know enough about the topic and therefore fail to include questions that tap into issues that are important in the particular topic (MacKinlay, 2001). The methods of qualitative research map out the territory, paint the picture, and provide a perspective on what areas need further study. Qualitative methods also allow the inductive construction of theory in new areas of learning and exploration. There is much still to be learned about aging and spirituality-and new methods of exploring this field are needed; therefore qualitative methods are important and appropriate to use in developing the area.

From a research perspective, it is possible to be quite rigorous in qualitative research. Rigor is obtained by continuing to collect data until no further themes arise (saturation), and by using a qualitative computer package (for example, QSR N6 or N-VIVO) to assist analysis of themes, through choice of words, sentences, or paragraphs to search for themes.

In-depth interviews and case studies are common ways of obtaining information in qualitative research.

1. In-Depth Interviews

In-depth interviews may provide rich data on a variety of topics. These interviews are usually used to obtain information about little known fields of study. Interviews in themselves may take various forms. Semi-structured or completely open interviews may range over a variety of topics, from narrative gerontology (e.g., Kenyon, Clark, & DeVries, 2001)-the telling of one's life story-to a focus on simply remembering episodes of earlier life. For example, questions can be as broad as meaning in later life (MacKinlay, 2001), or more focused and structured, to ask about the person's coping styles in stress management. In this paper, the focus will be on the broader approach. In the context of in-depth interviews with older adults, there are a number of terms used that may be unclear in meaning, for example, reminiscence, reminiscence therapy, and spiritual reminiscence. Reminiscence simply means to go back over earlier life (Coleman, 1994). Reminiscence therapy (Haight & Webster, 1995) is applying reminiscence as a therapy, while spiritual reminiscence is reminiscence that connects with the deeper aspects of life-meaning, and for those who have a faith, this involves how they have worked out this faith in their life journeys. Spiritual autobiography is similar to spiritual reminiscence, but consists of writing one's life story with the focus on the spiritual dimension. A spiritual autobiography has the advantage of allowing the individual to go back over the writing and reflect upon it, perhaps sharing it with another person. Thus reminiscence can be used in a research context, as an activity, or as therapy.

Interviews may be valuable ways of learning about the time and the characteristics of individuals and the way they see their lives in retrospect. Reminiscence is an essential way of moving through ageing and coming to terms with that final stage of life. It is a spiritual task of ageing (MacKinlay, 2001), and according to Erikson (1986) can lead a person to a sense of integrity rather than despair.

In recent years the importance of narrative, spiritual reminiscence and life review have been acknowledged. The story will necessarily be coloured by the meaning of people's individual stories, as understood and told by them. Where life review is used, each story is unique, being influenced by individual life history, education, health and cohort. In recent work with people who have dementia, a number of those interviewed, began by saying, 'I'm only an ordinary person, I don't have anything special to say' (MacKinlay, Trevitt, & Hobart, 2002). Once assured of the importance of their individual and unique story, these elderly people with dementia did have stories to share, just as the rest of us do. In-depth interviews focusing on the spiritual dimension were used by MacKinlay to construct a model of spiritual tasks and process of aging (MacKinlay, 2001). The model sets a framework for spiritual development and care, particularly in later life.

2. Case Studies

Case studies have become popular in recent years, with an increased interest developing in spiritual autobiographies. Case studies are classically a study of one person in-depth. The case study may consist of interviews, journals, and diaries. These form a valuable way of studying religion and spirituality that may be used by pastoral carers and therapists. An example of this is found in McFadden's (1999) work.

3. Qualitative Research with a Small Group of People (Focus Groups)

Focused discussions with small groups can provide a very effective method of finding ways of learning about religion and spirituality. See for example, Eisenhandler (2003) and Ramsey and Blieszner (1999), MacKinlay, Trevitt, and Hobart (2002), and Krause, Chatters, Meltzer, and Morgan (2000).

B. Correlational Studies

Correlation studies are conducted to see whether two (or more) variables are related, not as in cause/effect, but whether as one increases, the other increases (positive correlation) or decreases (negative correlation). For example, is being more religious in later life related to more or less depression? Correlations range between +1.00 and −1.00. More complex studies with many variables related in a number of hypothesized ways (e.g., as moderators or mediators of relationships among variables), employ statistical tests that include multiple regression and structural equation modeling. Correlation provides a measure of how variables are associated; it cannot give a measure of causality.

C. Experimental Studies

These are rarely used to study religiousness and spirituality. This is largely because experimental studies designs require one or more treatment groups and control groups. The nature of religion means that it is not possible to randomly assign persons to groups; for example, one cannot make people "religious" or "non-religious," although one can employ quasi-experimental methods in which people are sorted according to pre-existing conditions.

D. Action Research

Action research makes a deliberate connection of empirical studies to social programs that promise to bring change into people's lives. This is a very valuable means of conducting research where people and their attitudes and values are concerned, thus lending itself to the study of older adults and spirituality. For example, Mowat and Ryan (2002) looked at whether or not providing health to older adults, with a spiritual base might be a more effective way of providing health care than a way that ignores the spiritual base. This research importantly uses links with health care providers to tap into practice issues. Mowat and Ryan went into Scottish communities and asked a question that is very much tied to public policy and to changes that may be made in people's lives.

WHAT MAKES ADULT DEVELOPMENTAL RESEARCH SPECIAL?

Time is a critical feature in research on aging and older adults. For example, are there changes in religion and the spiritual dimension as people grow older? Do people become more or less religious as they age? Are older people more aware of the spiritual dimension of life? Neugarten (1968) found an increasing interiority in people from mid life onwards and perhaps this is associated with increasing interest in religion. For instance, in studies of death anxiety, some studies have shown very different levels between younger and older people, with older people tending to have lower death anxiety.

Studies of adult development and aging are looking at three fundamental effects:

1. *Aging effects:* These result from underlying processes (biological, social, psychological, and spiritual) that occur within the person with the passage of time.
2. *Cohort effects:* These are due to the experiences unique to a particular generation. It is important to consider what are the unique experiences of each cohort of people, based on the fact that they were born into a certain society with particular religious practices and beliefs.
3. *Time of measurement effects:* These result from social, environmental, historical or other events that occur when the data are collected. For example, results of studies of older adults might differ if religion and spirituality were measured in the 1960s when these dimensions were little spoken of, compared to the last decade when spirituality in particular was widely discussed.

KINDS OF RESEARCH DESIGNS USED TO STUDY
RELIGION AND AGING

1. *Cross sectional.* This design compares older people to younger people on the same variable, that is, a study of *age differences.* An important consideration in these studies is *confound* of age and cohort. In other words, one cannot be certain whether the results are due to the age differences or to cohort effects.

Cross-sectional studies are the most common design used in this research and many examples could be cited. The design may compare the one or more variables in different age groups at one point in time. One example is Toussaint, Williams, Musick, and Everson (2001). This study found that middle aged and older adults showed higher levels of forgiveness of others and feeling forgiven by God than younger adults; forgiveness of others was more strongly related to mental health in middle aged and older adults than for young adults. But, we cannot know whether different views of forgiveness are because of age or because persons of different ages experience different cohort influences and ways of thinking about the world. Religious attendance at 60 years of age may be higher because the 60-year-old persons have always been more "religious."

2. *Longitudinal.* Research using this design observes the same people over a period of time, thus noting *age change* within the same people. In longitudinal studies, the possible *confound* occurs because one cannot be certain the results occur because of the age of the participants and the time of measurement. Longitudinal studies of religiousness and spirituality include the following: Atchley (1997), Blazer and Palmore (1976), Kirkpatrick (1997), Markides, Levin, and Ray (1987), Shand (2000), and Wink and Dillon (2002).

3. *Time lag.* This design compares people of a particular age and cohort at one point in time, with the same aged people of a different cohort at another point in time, that is, a study of *cohort differences.* For example, the study might be of 70 year olds in 1980 with the same measures of 70 year olds repeated in 2000. *In this design, the confound* is cohort and time of measurement. Time lag studies could provide much important information about cohort differences. For example, will the religiosity and spirituality of contemporary middle aged baby boomers resemble that of middle

aged persons in 2030? Many of the studies of religion, spirituality, and aging that we rely upon today will need to be repeated for the next cohort.

How Can the Confounds Be Eliminated?

Complex designs that examine multiple cross-sectional, longitudinal, and time-lag comparisons avoid the confounds described above. These three designs (and their combination in more complex designs) can use either quantitative or qualitative data. The remainder of this article describes one project that employed a qualitative approach to research in ageing and spirituality.

AN EXAMPLE OF A QUALITATIVE RESEARCH PROJECT

One of the challenges in aged care currently is how to facilitate quality of life for people who have dementia. In Australia it is estimated there will be an increase of 254% in prevalence of dementia in the period 1995-2041 (Henderson & Jorm, 1998). Quite apart from the need to find a cure for Alzheimer's disease, it is important to gain some kind of understanding of what the experience of dementia is for those who experience it, so that effective strategies for care may be designed. Questionnaires to gauge quality of life and need for interventions cannot be designed for use in this area until researchers have some knowledge of what the issues are for people who have dementia.

In one study (MacKinlay, 2001) a Spiritual Health Inventory was used to assess spiritual health in older people. This inventory had been designed by Highfield (1981), assisted by a panel of a professor of psychology and assistant director of a counselling centre on a religiously-affiliated university campus, an assistant professor of Bible at the same institution with particular interest in needs of the dying person, and a minister completing a Masters degree in religion. However, there was no input from the target audience into the design of the questionnaire. Application of this Spiritual Health Inventory (SHI) (MacKinlay, 2001) could account for only 30.1 percent (by factor analysis) of the variance and was thus too low to accept as being a means of explanation for the level of spiritual health of these older people. When the results of the questionnaire using factor analysis were compared with the six themes identified through in-depth interviews of the same sample of older people, there was no connection between the six themes and the results of the SHI.

Thus, an assessment tool designed by a panel that does not include the target audience may fail to ask questions that are relevant and important to these people. At best this is misleading, as practitioners may think they are addressing certain aspects of need, but, unknown to them, the questionnaire does not even seek the information they really need to inform practice. This clearly illustrates the importance of undertaking exploratory studies in fields where little previous research has been done (Glaser & Strauss, 1967; Strauss & Corbin, 1990, MacKinlay, 2001). This will then provide a basis for theory from which to inform practice.

The best way to develop knowledge of how dementia affects those who live with it is to ask them. If this is not done, pastoral and health professionals may fail to assess for the relevant issues and problems that these people live with, because they do not know what questions are important to ask. It is only by asking the people themselves, by inquiring of their lived experience, that others, who do not experience the condition or life situation, can be enlightened. Grounded theory (Glaser & Strauss, 1967; Strauss & Corbin, 1990) provides a way to find the questions, that can then allow an examination of the possible answers to those questions. Theory can be built from the data, using an inductive approach. This may then lead to further studies using other methodologies (e.g., surveys); it may also provide enough evidence for developing assessment instruments for use in practice.

An Example of the Application of Grounded Theory

A pilot study, "The Search for Meaning: Quality of life for the person with dementia" (MacKinlay, Trevitt, & Hobart, 2002), examined the process of spiritual reminiscence and how this may be used therapeutically in working with people who have dementia. The project aimed to refine methodology in research into dementia, a critical area for investigation to improve quality of life for those living with dementia and their carers. The project was conducted with residents from two nursing homes and hostels for elderly people in two cities.

Project objectives were to examine how people experience dementia, explore how meaning and quality of life can be achieved by and for people who have dementia and to explore the concept of personhood and respect for persons with dementia. The study also examined strategies used by people who have dementia to overcome social and spiritual isolation.

The project employed phenomenological and grounded theory methods, using small groups, individual interviews and participant observation. In total, 22 people took part in the study. The groups met weekly for six weeks or for five months. Demographic data were collected prior to commencement and behaviour ratings were undertaken prior to group commencement and weekly, before and after each group session.

Grounded theory is particularly useful where little is known of a subject and there is a need to build up theory. Its advantages in ageing and spirituality are, first, it does not impose a structure on the participants. That is, they are able to respond to the things that are on their minds, the things that are important to them, rather than following the agenda of a researcher. This was done within the framework of the individual in-depth interviews, followed by joining a small group with weekly facilitated meetings in spiritual reminiscence.

Application of Grounded Theory in This Study

Due to the sensitive nature of the area of study, ethics clearance was obtained from the administering university and the industry partners (aged care facilities) in the study. Potential participants were approached by independent persons with a letter of explanation about the study and those willing to participate signed consent, where there was any concern of the ability of potential participants to give informed consent due to cognitive decline, their next of kin also signed the consent form.

The participants were then interviewed in-depth using a format (see Table 1) asking where they found deepest meaning in life, and following a process of exploring their spiritual dimension. This included exploration of joyful and sad life experiences, the hard things in life, the image they held of God (if they held one), church and religious attendance, relationships, transcendence and hope.

By using the Mini Mental State Examination (MMSE) participants were placed in groups according to their cognitive abilities, aiming not to have too great a range of cognitive competencies in any one group. The size of the group varied according to the ability of group members to communicate; those with greater difficulties were placed in smaller groups. Group size varied from two to six. The groups then met weekly for either six weeks or for five months. Earlier work of Yale (1995) used six week groups, but some people using six week groups have found that the longer term group may be more beneficial.

TABLE 1. The Questions Used in the In-Depth Interviews

1. What gives greatest meaning to your life now?
2. Looking back over your life:
   What do you remember with joy?
   What do you remember with sadness?

3. What are/have been the best things about relationships in your life?
   Use this as a starting point for exploring relationships with the group.
   Think of a number of questions, such as who visits them, who do they miss? Who have they been especially close to?

4. What things do you worry about?
   Do you feel you can talk to anyone about things that trouble you?
   What gives you hope now?

5. What are the hardest things in your life now?
6. What's it like growing older?
7. What's it like living here?

8. Do you have an image of God or some sense of a deity or otherness? If so, can you tell me about this image?
9. What are your earliest memories of church, mosque, temple or other worship?

10. Do you take part in any religious/spiritual activities? e.g., attend church services, Bible or other religious readings, prayer, meditation?
11. How can we help you to find meaning now?

Analysis of the Data

The in-depth interviews and each of the weekly group sessions were taped, transcribed and analysed using NUD*IST qualitative computer based package, employing the concepts of grounded theory. This method of analysis allows large amounts of narrative to be classified and examined to find the themes and categories from within the data. In this process the study participants are central to the outcomes of the study because it is their words that are analysed, not the preconstructed words of the researchers. This process recognises the validity of participants as experts on their own life stories. The categories identified from the data are listed in Table 2.

As well, INTERACT Behaviour Rating Scale (Baker & Dowling, 1995) was administered to each participant before and after each group session to measure any effect of participation in the groups. The INTERACT Scale was useful in the study as it provided another parameter of observation, and comparisons could be made of the groups (within group and between groups) from week to week and of the individuals in the groups. Although this was a pilot study with small numbers (22 participants) there were significant findings for single behav-

TABLE 2. Qualitative Data: Major Categories in the Data

Meaning in life Image of God Joy Relationship (see separate category) relationship almost synonymous with meaning	Response to meaning Attending church Faith Prayer Meditation
Transcendence of disabilities and loss Being sad Disabilities Humour Laughter and humour Growing older Hardest things in life Memory and memory loss Worry, anxiety	Coming to final meanings I'm just an ordinary person Wisdom
Relationship and intimacy Greatest meaning through relationship Being lonely Diversional therapist communication style Grief	Hope Hope and Fear

iour ratings using paired t-tests. There were 12 paired behaviours so a Bonferroni correction was carried out arriving at significant (at .025 one tailed t-test) for three different categories of happy-content, attentive/responding, and did things from own initiative. These changes from before to after the group sessions were positive. It is emphasised however that the main focus of the groups was on the use of spiritual reminiscence and in finding what themes and categories were important for these people with dementia.

What Can Be Learned from Such a Study?

By nature, a qualitative study is an exploratory study. It is a first look at the scene. It does not foreclose on questions that need to be asked. It may illuminate questions that the researcher had not thought about before exploring this area. In this study, the main findings related to communication styles of the group facilitators, and to the need for close connection with the participants in their everyday lives.

The issues raised in this study are at the heart of what it is to be human. People with dementia find it hard at times to communicate effectively. All staff in aged care facilities need to be aware of the kinds of difficulties these people experience and be willing to support them in respectful caring environments. Qualitative methods can be used to open up areas of practice that have not been previously studied and where change of practice is needed. Qualitative studies respect the people they study and give people, particularly vulnerable people, a voice.

CONCLUSION

This paper has explored ways of studying the relationship between ageing, religion and spirituality. It has outlined past and current directions in methods of research in this rapidly developing field. Examples have been used to highlight issues for practice and research. Best practice in aged care can only be developed on the basis of sound research projects and discerning, critical practitioners. The example of the study of spiritual reminiscence and small groups for people with dementia showed one way in which different research methods may be used in combination to strengthen the findings of research. This pilot study on dementia has allowed examination of the study design and refinement of this for a subsequent successful grant application.[1]

NOTE

1. MacKinlay, E. B, Trevitt, C., and Coady, M. 'Finding meaning in the experience of dementia: The place of spiritual reminiscence work.' Australian Research Council Linkage Grant 2002-2004.

REFERENCES

Atchley, R. C. (1997). The subjective importance of being religious and its effect on health and morale 14 years later. *Journal of Aging Studies, 11*, 131-141.
Baker, R., & Dowling, Z. (1995). Interact. A new measure of response to multisensory environments. Research Publications. Bournemouth: Research and Development support Unit, Institute of Health and Community Studies, Bournemouth University.
Blazer, D., & Palmore, E. (1976). Religion and aging in a longitudinal panel. *The Gerontologist, 16*, 82-85.

Coleman, P. G. (1994). 'Reminiscence within the study of ageing: The social significance of story.' In J. Bornat (Ed.), *Reminiscence Reviewed*. Buckingham: Open University Press. 8-20.

Eisenhandler, S. A. (2003). *Keeping the faith in late life*. New York: Springer.

Erikson, E, H. Erikson, J. M., & Kivnick, H. Q. (1986). *Vital Involvement in Old Age*. New York: W. W. Norton & Co.

Glaser, B. G., & Strauss, A. L. (1967). *The Discovery of Grounded Theory: Strategies for Qualitative Research*. Chicago: Aldine Atherton.

Haight, B. K., & Webster, J. D. (ed) (1995). *The Art and Science of Reminiscence: Theory, Research, Methods, and Application*. Washington, DC: Taylor & Francis.

Henderson, A. S., & Jorm, A. F. (1998). *Dementia in Australia*. Aged and Community Care Division; Department of Health and Family Services. Canberra.

Highfield, M. F. (1981). *Oncology Nurses' Awareness of their Patients' Spiritual Needs and Problems*. Unpublished Thesis, Little Rock: University of AR for Medical Sciences.

Kenyon, G., Clark, P., & DeVries, G. (eds.). (2001). *Narrative gerontology: Theory, research, and practice*. New York: Springer.

Kirkpatrick, L. (1997). A longitudinal study of changes in religious belief and behavior as a function of individual differences in adult attachment style. *Journal for the Scientific Study of Religion, 36*, 207-217.

Krause, N., Chatters, L., M., Meltzer, T., & Morgan, D. L. (2000). Using focus groups to explore the nature of prayer in late life. *Journal of Aging Studies, 14*, 191-212.

McFadden, S. H. (1999). Surprised by joy and burdened by age: The journal and letters of John Casteel. In L. E. Thomas & S. A. Eisenhandler (eds.), *Religion, belief, and spirituality in late life* (pp. 137-149). New York: Springer.

McFadden, S. H., Brennan, M., & Patrick, J. H. (2002). *New directions in the study of late life religiousness and spirituality*. New York: The Haworth Press, Inc.

MacKinlay, E.B., Trevitt, C., & Hobart, S. (2002). *The Search for Meaning: Quality of life for the person with dementia*. University of Canberra Collaborative Grant, 2001. Unpublished Project Report, February 2002.

MacKinlay, E.B. (2001). *The spiritual dimension of ageing*. London: Jessica Kingsley.

Markides, K.S., Levin, J.S., & Ray, L. A. (1987). Religion, aging, and life satisfaction: An eight-year, three-wave longitudinal study. *The Gerontologist, 27*, 660-665.

Mowat, H., & Ryan, D. (2002). Spiritual issues in health and social care: Practice into policy? *Journal of Religious Gerontology, 14*(1). 51-67.

Neugarten, B. L. (1968). 'Adult personality: Toward a psychology of the life cycle.' In B.L. Neugarten (Ed.), *Middle Age and Aging: A Reader in Social Psychology*. Chicago: The University of Chicago Press.

Ramsey, J. L., & Blieszner, R. (1999). *Spiritual resiliency in older women: Models of strength for challenges through the life span*. Thousand Oaks, CA: Sage.

Reker, G. T. (1995). Quantitative and qualitative methods. In M. A. Kimble, S. H. McFadden, J. W. Ellor, & J. J. Seeber (eds.), *Aging, spirituality, and religion: A handbook* (pp. 568-588). Minneapolis: Fortress Press.

Shand, J. D. (2000). The effects of life experiences over a 50-year period on the certainty of belief and disbelief in God. *The International Journal for the Psychology of Religion, 10*, 85-100.

Strauss, A., & Corbin, J. (1990). *Basics of Qualitative Research: Grounded Theory Procedures and Techniques*. Newbury Park: SAGE Publications.

Toussaint, L. L., Williams, D. R., Musick, M. A., & Everson, S. A. (2001). Forgiveness and health: Age differences in a U.S. probability sample. *Journal of Adult Development, 8,* 249-257.

Wink, P., & Dillon, M. (2002). Spiritual development across the adult life course: Findings from a longitudinal study. *Journal of Adult Development, 9,* 79-94.

Yale, R. (1995). *Developing support groups for individuals with early stage Alzheimer's Disease planning, implementation, and evaluation.* Baltimore: Health Professions Press.

Spiritual and Pastoral Care Approaches for Helping Older Adults with Depression

John White, MEd

SUMMARY. Pastoral and Spiritual Care approaches to the reduction of depression in residential aged care facilities are considered. They are examined through specific one-to-one pastoral care, through a pastoral care person in the team approach to care and through a one-to-many relationship for group spiritual and religious activities. The suggestions in this article are offered as extensions to a manual, *Challenge Depression*, on managing depression in residential aged care as a way of including pastoral and spiritual care as part of an integrated approach and as part of a stand alone approach of pastoral care. *[Article copies available for a fee from The Haworth Document Delivery Service: 1-800-HAWORTH. E-mail address: <docdelivery@haworthpress.com> Website: <http://www.HaworthPress.com> © 2004 by The Haworth Press, Inc. All rights reserved.]*

KEYWORDS. Pastoral care, depression, ageing, residential aged care, spiritual tasks of ageing, holistic care

---

The Rev. John White is Rector, St John's Anglican Church, Bairnsdale, Australia, and Academic Associate, School of Theology, Charles Sturt University.

[Haworth co-indexing entry note]: "Spiritual and Pastoral Care Approaches for Helping Older Adults with Depression." White, John. Co-published simultaneously in *Journal of Religious Gerontology* (The Haworth Pastoral Press, an imprint of The Haworth Press, Inc.) Vol. 16, No. 3/4, 2004, pp. 91-107; and: *Spirituality of Later Life: On Humor and Despair* (ed: Rev. Elizabeth MacKinlay) The Haworth Pastoral Press, an imprint of The Haworth Press, Inc., 2004, pp. 91-107. Single or multiple copies of this article are available for a fee from The Haworth Document Delivery Service [1-800-HAWORTH, 9:00 a.m. - 5:00 p.m. (EST). E-mail address: docdelivery@haworthpress.com].

The Commonwealth of Australia Department of Health and Ageing commissioned the Hammond Group to look at and seek ways to manage the problem of depression of residents in aged care facilities and in 2001, *Challenge Depression* (Commonwealth of Australia Department of Health and Ageing, 2001) a manual and video were produced to assist staff to identify and reduce depression of people in their care.

Over recent years a growing body of literature has developed in pastoral care of older people and the spiritual tasks that are an essential aspect of ageing (Moberg, 2001a, MacKinlay, 2001b, Bratt, 2001, Koenig & Weaver, 1997b). Some of the studies specifically note pastoral care as an important aspect of care in reducing depression in older people; examples are Koenig and Weaver (1997a) and McFadden (1995). An objective observation of the approaches suggested in the *Challenge Depression Manual* is that it does not include pastoral care as an approach, either as one integrated into an overall team care plan or as one-on-one care basis. The Manual refers to work which enabled statistical quantification of depressive disorders in aged care facilities. It indicates that up to 60% of residents could be mildly to severely depressed and that more than 50% of these residents were described as being depressed prior to admission.

The high incidence of depression is unacceptable on any measure, especially as existing treatment, care plans, activities and opportunities for serving others that reduce depression for older people in aged care facilities are available. The manual outlines twelve approaches based on research, reported experience, available personnel and program resources, and suggested team approaches.

The introduction to the *Challenge Depression Manual* notes, "This manual does not claim to be complete. There are many more chapters that could be and perhaps should be added to it" (p. 10), and it is from this observation that motivation for a pastoral care approach comes. Fleming (2002) notes various findings that link spirituality positively with improved mental health. In reference to practice in Australia he notes that there is less emphasis on spiritual support than on diversional activities with reluctance in many facilities to use pastoral care workers.

Holistic care is partly informed and improved through responding to the established connections between spiritual life and well-being and the older person's ability and capacity to thrive (Mowat & Ryan, 2002). Hence consideration of pastoral and spiritual care as an integral and important element in the reduction of depression in residential facilities (Fleming, 2002).

At the heart of this pastoral care approach is the concept of the human person as a complex interaction and interdependence of body, spirit, mind and feelings and that no particular aspect of the human person can be identified or cared for separately or in isolation. The work of Mowat and Ryan (2002) in describing *Spirited Scotland* offers good support for the concept that "successful ageing could be defined as a journey which is more spiritual than physical" (p. 62). Care of the inner-being, the human spirit is therefore an integral aspect of holistic care and in challenging depression there is a need to identify aspects of pastoral and spiritual care that will assist in the reduction of depressive symptoms, and work towards healing depression.

A HEALTHY SPIRITUAL ATTITUDE TO THE ILLNESS CALLED DEPRESSION

In the holistic view of the human being, spiritual functioning has at least equal relevance to the physical, mental and emotional functioning of our lives and cannot be isolated from the other components. Depression cannot be treated simply by changing the chemical balance in the physical aspect of the mind, nor can psychotherapeutic approaches be offered in isolation, nor can the spiritual be isolated as the only component to be treated for depression, but in caring for a person holistically the spiritual aspects of the person's life cannot be ignored.

The work described here refers to the management of mild depressive symptoms, those which last at least two weeks and include sadness, loss of interest in life's activities or pleasures, low self-esteem, changes in sleeping and eating patterns, poor attention and concentration, and a negative outlook on the world as defined in the *Challenge Depression Manual.*

There is a sense of ill-being about this list of symptoms, and there seems to be a need to nourish the inner-being to build up well-being. For example a feeling and experience of despair is ill-being, the opposite of which is hope; feeling isolated is overcome with love; sadness is the ill-feeling that has its diminishment in joy. Peace is the well-being experience opposed to anxiety and creativity is that which overcomes boredom. Hope, love, joy, peace and creativity are qualities of experience of the human spirit that are life-giving-the attributes of despair, isolation, sadness, anxiety and boredom are qualities of experience of the human spirit that are life-denying; they sound like those experienced by a person suffering from depression.

SPIRITUAL TASKS OF AGEING

Elizabeth MacKinlay (2001b) has identified six spiritual themes of ageing and a corresponding six identifiable spiritual tasks of ageing.

Ultimate meaning comes from our need for meaning making (MacKinlay, 2001b) and experiences of making meaning through the events and vicissitudes of life. The need is met in a meaning that transcends human life; in a transcendent energy or power or being. Attending to a person's spirituality gives the opportunity for continuing meaning and purpose to a person's life and nourishes the inner being. Inability to find meaning is an unsettling experience and a source of restlessness; well-being is restored when meaning of an event is made, when what is perplexing is grounded or what confuses is clarified. It seems that well-being is about happiness while ill-being is about depression.

Depression is an illness that clouds some of the ability to respond to what is seen by the person as the Ultimate Meaning of life. Ill-being may be experienced in the despair, anxiety and boredom coming from the illness called depression that separates the person from the desire and hence the ability to respond to the Ultimate Meaning of life.

As people live through the fourth quarter of life there are many changes, losses and disabilities that are to be transcended. Transcending losses involves grieving, a natural and spiritual journey from the person's prior circumstances to the person's state of well-being and new meaning in life. Depression is a natural emotional response in the journey of transcendence of loss; it may become an illness when the journey of grief is stalled.

Exploring and finding meaning in and for a person's own death is a spiritual task expressed in terms, religious experiences and symbols that have been part of their experience. Learning how to die is certainly a spiritual task and it is different from wanting to die or feeling like dying or even choosing suicide. Well-being is about learning how to die; ill-being is about wanting to die. It seems like one is about happiness, the other about depression; one is about thriving, the other about emptiness.

A healthy relationship builds on trust and it is in this sort of relationship that people will be able to take off their masks. If older people with depression are to be able to disclose thoughts, opinions, fears and feelings that are very important and sensitive to them, then they can best do so in an environment in which there is no fear of judgment, criticism or condemnation. In developing intimacy, time spent together is essential.

In a life-time of forming, maintaining and growing in relationship conflict occurs because it is part of relating. In some cases the conflict remains unresolved and is a quite unhealthy influence on well-being. The resolution, having time for amendment and enjoying it and living out new life resulting from forgiveness and reconciliation are aspects of this spiritual task of ageing. Intimacy with the Ultimate Meaning, extending these notions of human intimacy, has the potential of a person becoming who they were created or formed to be.

Hope is an assurance there is something more in the midst of the journey of ageing (Jewell, 1999). Hope is an encouragement that there is more of what is better. It seems that without hope there is despair and anguish. Having a strong spiritual life, described by MacKinlay (2001a) as coming from the six spiritual tasks of ageing seems to provide a framework for dealing with despair.

Koenig and Weaver (1997a) list twenty-five major psychological and spiritual needs of older adults and in doing so they have provided several foci for challenging depression in older people. Included as needs are: meaning and purpose, sense of usefulness, vision, hope, support in coping with loss, change and death of loved ones, adapting to increasing dependency and difficult circumstances, personal dignity, expression of feelings, expression of gratitude, continuity with the past and preparation for death and dying. In relation to God, Koenig and Weaver (1997b) observe the need to experience and be certain that God exists and is on their side with unconditional love. They also refer to a number of religious needs which include praying alone, with others, and for others, reading and being inspired by Scripture, worshiping God, individually and corporately and to love and serve God. In relation to community, spiritual needs are for fellowship with others, loving and serving others and being able to confess, be forgiven and to forgive others.

A PASTORAL CARE APPROACH TO IDENTIFYING AND REDUCING DEPRESSION PRIOR TO ADMISSION

The stress and grief associated with the significant transitional period in their life moving from community to residential care is well recognized in the *Challenge Depression Manual*. These people are leaving a neighbourhood and special supportive friends; they are leaving their own home with its family gatherings, memories, spaces; a garden perhaps is left behind, the place where they could find peace and solitude; and perhaps there is a pet they have to say goodbye to; they are leaving what is familiar to them. There may be a reality or a perceived reality that they "are being put away." Older people moving from independent living, even if it has been supported by community and family care, feel that they are about to lose their independence. More than that, their advancing disabilities, poorer health and cognitive impairment remind them of what they have lost, wondering where all their years have gone and even that their ageing bodies remind them of death being closer. Adjusting to, overcoming and accepting these losses and anticipated losses is what the grieving process is about and part of the process naturally includes times of depression or deep sadness.

Of course, grief is not the only cause of depression at this transitional period. The years of isolation and loneliness may have contributed to the depressive disorder, so may illnesses and disabilities, disappointments, abuse, unresolved issues, abandonment by the family, mental illnesses and unfulfilled dreams.

It may be time, if it has not already been done, to create a memory box (Treetops, 1999). A memory box, about the size of a shoe box, but more sturdy and certainly painted and decorated, contains all sorts of collectibles from the life and belongings of the resident. The collection of sensory stimuli connect the life of the resident to their past and as it is compiled there may be an assurance that there will be triggers for memories of their life.

FUNCTIONS OF PASTORAL CARE

In the first instance, *pastoral care offers the gift of time and listening* for this depressed older person in the transition of moving to residential care. It is care that for practical and time constraints is not readily available from other carers in the person's life. The pastoral carer offers the single gift of being fully present to the person with depression. Pastoral care gives an opportunity for the older person to be heard, to actually have someone listen without judgment, criticism, advice, censure, reproof or with patronizing or condescending attitudes. As pastoral care is the care of being there, timing is very significant and it depends very much on building an authentic relationship of trust, constancy and unconditional positive regard and this takes time. This care happens when the relationship is approached with an attitude of unconditional positive regard for the older person (Rogers, 1965).

The care of religious presence provides a ministry of prayer, readings, sacraments and a rite of passage. The choice is with the older person as to what they want in this ministry, they may choose to have the faith community leader as the one who leads the prayer and/or sacramental pastoral service with a voluntary pastoral carer being there as personal support. It is a very good time to have the family with the older person for these prayers. This form of religious and spiritual care may bring a sense of peace and assurance. It may emotionally and spiritually uplift the person to know that others are praying. The voice given to the hope that is present may generate hope, confidence and lessen the burden for the older person facing the transition (Moberg, 2001a). The essential aspect to be aware of in this care is that prayer and religious support needs to be caringly offered in response to the older person's individual religious style. Through religious practices and forms of prayer and meditation many people have found healing, relief, hope and the ability to accept things happening which are out of their control (Ai et al., 2002). The spiritual tasks of acceptance, adjusting, time for amendment, gratitude and celebration are often helped by prayer for people with faith (Moberg, 1994).

In the case of the depressed older person not being a practising member of a faith community it is not appropriate to assume that it would be helpful for the older person about to leave their home to have a prayer said, or have the minister call around. What is appropriate is to listen to the messages coming through, for example there may be sacred spaces and memories and the person may refer to past experiences with a faith community.

The *care of spiritual companionship* is the care that accompanies the older person as they seek to make sense of what is happening in terms of the bigger picture of their life and the bigger picture of a power that is greater than them and greater than life. In the transition to residential care the elements of change may be felt in terms of emptiness and loss of spirits. Overcoming the lethargy that is part of depression in this transition is often helped by the spiritual companion constantly walking with, not carrying or not crowding out, just being there at the right time offering the safe space for the untangling of emotions, becoming spiritually aware and surfacing new thoughts.

A faith community provides a range of care other than the religious presence. Having a community of faith may increase well-being gained through friendship, mutual support, shared ideas and having a sense of identity. It is in community that each member has the opportunity to further develop as a person, even at the transition time from independent living to residential living. There is a sense of belonging in a faith community. In a faith community there is a rich range of abilities and experiences that can offer physical, intellectual, spiritual, and emotional support for the older person about to enter residential care.

Pastoral care maintains *the care of faith community* for those in the faith community. There are some older people who are steeped in the traditions of their faith community. They require the spiritual nourishment and uplift, worship response opportunities to their Ultimate Meaning and connection to the symbols and signs of their religious practices. Pastoral care may be able to arrange for the continuity of provision of these services for the older person entering residential care. The pastoral carer is able to join the resident and participate in these religious practices.

Pastoral care offered leading up to and during the transition to residential care is care that has the potential to continue into the environment of the residential facility. While so many changes are occurring in the life of the older person, pastoral care, if it is appropriately organised is able to provide a constant that otherwise may not be there.

PASTORAL CARE AND MEDICAL MANAGEMENT: A TEAM APPROACH TO CARE

The use of medication for the management and healing of depression is strictly the domain of the resident's doctor. Pastoral care does not include any commentary about the efficacy of medication for the reduction of depressive symptoms. However, because medication is administered for the reduction of the symptoms, it may be found that the resident is more open to pastoral care as part of the program of holistic care for the reduction of symptoms and the healing of depression. The *Challenge Depression Manual* notes that medication is usually not administered in isolation, but rather as part of other approaches.

Pastoral care, in consultation with the team, has roles in the overall assessment and care plan for the resident in the team approach to holistic care. The team may be reminded of the multifaceted nature of a person that includes the human spirit and the resident's search for meaning. Grief counselling may be made more possible due to the reduced symptoms of depression and the pastoral carer companions the resident through the spiritual journey of grief. Pastoral care becomes a more effective element of care as the medication gives clarity of mind and an attitude enabling better working through regrets, needs for amendment of life and forgiveness and bringing to mind unresolved issues in life. In the team approach the pastoral carer will be able to advance the spiritual care of residents, informing the process with a knowledge of the spiritual tasks of ageing (MacKinlay, 2001a). Awareness of the presence of a resilient and 'defiant' aspect of the human person, the person's spirit is useful. Kimble (2001) observes that for many it appears that the crisis in old age is a crisis of meaning and Close (2000) adds that it is important to identify the unquestioned core beliefs the resident has in arriving at life's meaning. Kimble (2001) sees that the ultimate answer to the question of meaning in old age would be for old age itself to offer the elderly something worthwhile for which to live. Kimble (2001) writes "Meaning-making at its core is a spiritual exercise." The use of symbols and ritual can be very valuable in assisting older adults who struggle with issues of integrity, dignity and meaning to get in touch with meaning and their spiritual selves.

DEVELOP DEPRESSION-SENSITIVE POLICIES AND PROCEDURES

The role of pastoral care in residential care is to be informative for the development of procedures and is an integral aspect of the procedures and practices. The establishment of a residential facility pastoral care committee may be necessary for the dual role of pastoral care in the depression sensitive policies and procedures. Depression sensitive policies and procedures based on 'person-centred' care (Kitwood, 1997) will include such considerations as allocation of quality relationship building and maintenance time to the older person and their family. Through appropriate procedures the resident is assisted in becoming informed about all aspects of care, from experiencing a trusting environment, to preventing isolation, to having a feeling of security and knowing that she is important and significant. Policies and procedures are formed out of an awareness of the 12 approaches outlined in the *Challenge Depression Manual* with additional awareness of pastoral and spiritual care.

A lifestyle plan designed for the resident to attend to the spiritual tasks of ageing becomes essential. In the development of depression-sensitive procedures and practices a simple recognition of the transition from independent living to residential care living in the form of rite of passage may be appropriate. The ritual may be based on a particular religious rite, or a particular set of circumstances, on feelings, gratitude and hopes, or as a healing process.

The procedures for meeting religious needs are important. It is totally insensitive and inappropriate for a resident to be taken out of a religious service to be given other forms of care. The practice demeans the value of pastoral care and ignores the holistic needs of the resident. The resident with depression may be seeking ways through religious and spiritual traditions to find hope, love, meaning, joy and trust and it further shakes the ways of handling depression if their religious practices are treated as being inconsequential. There are many people involved in the arrangements for a Religious Service, many of them busy people who have made the effort to be available, and they come together at the pre-arranged time.

Attendance at and participation in a religious service of worship, prayer or teaching is an occasion for a resident to receive soul nourishment. The experience for the resident may be unique, personal, private, life-giving and life-changing, all adding up to a special experience for the residence. If a resident suffering from depression chooses to attend a religious service then the special nature of the experience may provide ways to manage, reduce or heal the depression. The common experience of worship and prayer may establish a pastoral care relationship that works towards the amelioration of the resident's depressed state.

Depression-sensitive procedures will ensure the availability of religious services from which to choose and will develop policies for unhurried access, uncluttered and private space and uninterrupted times for worship, prayer and other religious services. As well as on-site religious services the attendance at community religious activities is to be encouraged where possible. Pastoral care often involves the sharing of private thoughts, feelings and disclosures that require a private place for the pastoral relationship to take place. The use of the resident's room is not always appropriate, neither is it appropriate to hunt around in the hope that a quiet spot can be found. The quiet place may be a designated meeting/interview room or a sacred space provided by the facility. A depression-sensitive policy will allocate such a space for unobtrusive use.

DESIGNATED SACRED SPACE

A sacred space is a dedicated multi-purpose room that is set aside for religious worship and prayer services, private meditation and prayer, group work studies and discussion groups, counselling, and listening groups. A sacred space may also be used for family gathering at time of a resident's illness or dying and death, a quiet place for a resident to be with a family member or friend, a place to be still and as a centre acknowledged as sacred and a reminder of the spiritual focus of each person and of care.

The sacred space should be sensitively and creatively provided with familiar symbols, ornaments, atmospheric décor, inviting furniture and seating. The sacred space provides a room that is noticeably different from any other space in the facility giving a sense of peace, transcendence and a touching of the inner being. This is both an important place for religious worship and prayer and a place where pastoral care relationships are developed. A depression-sensitive practice acknowledges the value of such a sacred retreat and safe place for residents with depression.

PASTORAL CARE FOR END OF LIFE ISSUES

The admission to residential aged care begins a period in life that usually ends with death or hospitalisation followed by death. In a society which denies death and ageing, old age and residential care can be quite confronting simply because it may be the first time death is confronted. The depressed older adult may very well be depressed because learning how to die has not been considered. The famous pioneer writer about death and dying, Elizabeth Kubler-Ross (1969) observed that the dying stage in our life may be experienced as the most profound growth event of our total life's experience. Death is unique in each lifetime and unique for each person, yet death is as much part of life as is birth, growing, maturation and dying. Even though there is mystery with death, part of growing older and integrating the experiences of ageing into a meaningful and healthy context is the need to share the feelings and thoughts about the process that is opening up into mystery of death.

The pastoral care offered to a depressed older person needs to include opportunities for the pastoral carer to listen to these feelings and thoughts and to assist the older person to express fears and uncertainties as a way of facing the many unsaid and unsayable attitudes about death.

Coming to terms with the final meanings of one's life is obviously quite complex, potentially threatening and does not follow a pre-defined sequence of steps. Yet, the process and the achievement of coming to terms with dying and death is so life giving and healing that pastoral care options should be offered for those suffering depression due to the realisation that the final stage of life has begun. Pastoral care may include offering the appropriate religious care in terms of liturgical practices, prayer, scripture readings, pronouncement of forgiveness, mysticism and meditation. Pastoral care may also encourage older adults to look at dying and death and to doubt as well to hope, to be angry as well as to love, to be anxious as well as to be peaceful, to feel isolated as well as to feel loved and to feel guilty as well as to feel forgiven. This gives the person 'room' to explore and not to feel confined by a doctrinal expectation; rather things are seen from different perspectives.

Pastoral care is care that offers a safe, non-critical and compassionate environment for doubts to be viewed, reviewed and reframed. Pastoral care involves journeying with the older person through their grief caused by actual losses and anticipated losses. Joanne Armatowski (2001) gives excellent advice about the benefits of support to the elderly in coming to terms with their dying and death. Having dignity, integrity and self-worth affirmed seems to be antithetical to depression.

In order to preserve their dignity, integrity and self-worth, the elderly need to know that others support them. The supportive task of others is simply to see the beauty that lies within, accept the truth of who and what they in essence are, and capture the goodness. Helping others, whenever possible, will strengthen and complete, rather than weaken and fragment, the lives of those who care (p. 76).

It is in a committed pastoral care relationship that the older adult in residential care is able to have access to others who alleviate loneliness, yet still encouraging aloneness. Loneliness is isolating and is about abandonment and boredom; aloneness is about being content with one-self and letting oneself be.

PASTORAL CARE FOR OVERCOMING FEAR OF THE "NURSING HOME"

Entering high care residential accommodation happens because the resident is becoming dependent on others for care, to the extent that appropriate care can no longer be delivered in their own home. For the new resident, pain and suffering, discomfort, cognitive impairment, losses of dignity and independence, mashed food and lifting machines are all bearing down as sources of fear. A depression-sensitive approach will encourage pastoral care of the resident as a constant complement to the other forms of care so that the resident has a listening and under-standing companion through the fears of this stage of ageing. The resident is in the "rest of living" (Simmons & Wilson, 2001) stage of life that is a potentially rich and engaged part of life even though it is also a time of dependence and frailty. An older person with depression entering this period of "rest of living" may be facing years of depression; likewise an adult without depression entering the "rest of living" may become depressed. Depression-sensitive procedures are necessary for the "rest of living" period so that diminishments are experienced without the person being diminished. It is a period of experiencing more of the ageing process, yet it is not necessary that the resident ceases self expression and relating to others.

CREATE A HAPPY, HELPFUL ENVIRONMENT

Approach 4 in the *Challenge Depression Manual* is about sustaining positive attitudes in residents through appropriate physical surroundings. The environment is an essential factor in the establishment and maintenance of any level of pastoral care. Pastoral care for residents with depression needs flexible use of space. Flexibility may be a difficult challenge for a depressed resident, but being involved in the challenge may assist in healing through the safe broadening of experiences. There are times when the pastoral care can be safely offered in open and public spaces-it is much like having a chat. At other times a private place is necessary as the resident wishes to work on issues that they may feel reluctant to speak of in public areas.

The pastoral care associated with broadening the social network begins with one-to-one relating in a familiar non-threatening environment for the resident using basic pastoral care skills. After inviting the resident and offering choice, the basic one-to-one pastoral care relationship may continue in less familiar environments. A characteristic of depression may be expressed in fear of anything new, or of the slightest challenge and the pastoral carer needs to be aware of this. The transition to a non-familiar environment is approached gently and sensitively. Perhaps just a short walk together in the facility may be the beginning. Whereas the resident's room may be the familiar environment, the pastoral care relationship taking place in the less familiar environment of the lounge room, for example, may be quite a challenge and big step for the older person with depression. The pastoral carer will have in mind the values associated with meeting in unfamiliar environments, but the journey towards this achievement is very much at the resident's own pace and direction. Beyond the small lounge room is a larger lounge room and a garden outside; and the craft room, the Sacred Space, the work shed and the street outside.

BE SENSITIVE TO CULTURAL ISSUES

Just as understanding cultural influences, networking, cultural activities and communication are important, it is also important to offer pastoral care that is culturally sensitive and culturally informed. Culturally sensitive pastoral care actually heightens the awareness that each person in aged care has a cultural heritage with cultural needs that each has in some ways individualised. However, pastoral care is basically dependent on establishing a familiar non-threatening environment for the resident. The pastoral carer needs to be very well informed about language, customs, mores, ways of communicating and religious traditions in order to be sensitive and respectful to and be empathic within the pastoral environment. Essential work is required in this field of pastoral care for residents with depression from various cultures and it will be a valuable resource for the pastoral care of residents in aged care suffering depression.

FINDING PURPOSE IN LIFE

Vaillant's (2002) evidence supports the psychologist Edmund Sanford, writing in 1902,

> The real secret of a happy old age [is] once more in service for others carried on to the end of life-a service which, on the one hand, give perennial interest to life by making the old man [or woman] a participant in the life of those around about him, and on the other, surrounds him with love in return. (p. 324)

A pastoral care approach to reducing depression then seems to need to include opportunities for the older person to serve others.

HELP PEOPLE TO BE THEMSELVES

Many of the symptoms indicating depression in an older adult work against the person engaging in life-affirming self selected activities and ways of doing things. In order for the depressed older person to realise more of their personal potential they need to become aware that the person they are being in depression is not who they actually are. The glimpses of ways of redefining themselves may come about through psychotherapy and/or medication. Further, healing from depression may be dependent on healthy choices, routines and options being available to further help the older person 'be themselves,' who they really can be. The ageing process, entering residential aged care, experiencing accumulated losses and listening to the gloomy predictions and expectations of others may lead the older person to a 'closed down' version of living. There may be a life-denying acceptance that there is no choice, and stuck in a routine defined by the facility, the resident has no more opportunity to develop as a person. Pastoral care seeks to look at other perspectives.

Some of the ways pastoral care can assist a person to be more of themselves include focussing on an older adult's inner well-being. This is intentionally finding joy even though there is sadness, finding hope even though there may be despair, finding love even though there may be isolation and anger, finding peace even though there may be anxiety and finding creativity when so much of life may be boring. Pastoral care offers a constant companionship as challenges are faced and feelings and reactions of the experiences of exercising choices are 'debriefed.' Pastoral care looks at ways of helping responses to grow out of reactions of the resident, especially as they work through the 'deaths' and resurrections that are part of life. The resident is assisted and encouraged in reflecting on and relating experiences to their spirituality and religion and with using prayer, meditation and sacred readings to help with a more life-giving response. The pastoral carer joins in with the celebration of new-life experiences, renewed "spring in the steps" and achievements as the rest of living takes on new meaning and fulfillment.

USING REMINISCENCE AND SPIRITUAL LIFE REVIEW AS AN APPROACH TO REDUCING DEPRESSION IN OLDER PEOPLE

Reminiscence, the process of recounting and interpreting past life events is known to be of great benefit to older people (Morgan, 1996). Pastoral care skills are needed when the reminiscence becomes, intentionally or naturally, a matter of life review that results in looking at assisting individuals deal with difficult times in their lives (Moberg, 2001b). During life review older people may take stock of their own lives, be helped with the spiritual tasks, be helped to get their experiences of life into the world view they have formed, find answers to the question of "what do I do with my remaining time," have opportunities to view the legacy they are leaving and provide a transmission of history, values and knowledge to the following generations. In life review the older person has opportunities to re-integrate unresoled griefs, conflicts, fears, guilts, frustrations, and broken relationships into a new perspective. Addressing the despair over their inability to come to terms with life and facing death and disappointment with what they had not achieved, or with what they had caused is difficult work but may be assisted by pastorally sensitive life review. Life review is also helpful for celebration of life and seeing the influence of the Transcendent. In pastoral care through life review, spiritual needs of an older person with depression may be addressed, reducing the depression. The spiritual needs of older people (Moberg, 2001b) matched to the symptoms of depression in older people through life review seems to be a very useful approach.

CONCLUSION

The paper has been a first attempt to extend the care of depressed adults in aged care facilities, as outlined in the *Challenge Depression Manual and Video* to the specific integration and addition of pastoral care. This attempt may be read in conjunction with other works like the *Spirited Scotland* program (Mowat & Ryan, 2002) and the ongoing work of the Hammond Group in the *Challenge Depression* (2001) program (Fleming, 2002) as part of the necessary work required in managing and reducing depression in people living in residential aged care facilities. A more far-reaching outcome of these specific issues may be that spiritual and pastoral care becomes a recognised, funded and essential aspect of holistic care of older frail adults. This calls for much more than this first attempt at extending *Challenge Depression*; it calls for concerted research, consolidating the descriptions of professional pastoral care, and an energetic and unrelenting representation to decision makers keeping in focus the holistic needs of the person who is to be cared for holistically.

REFERENCES

Ai, A.L., Peterson, C., Bolling, S.F. & Koenig, H. (2002). Private prayer and optimism in middle-aged and older patients awaiting cardiac surgery. *The Gerontologist*, *44*, 1, 70-81.

Armatowski, J. (2001). Attitudes toward death and dying among persons in the fourth quarter of life. In D.O. Moberg (Ed.), *Aging and spirituality: Spiritual dimensions of aging theory, research practice and policy*. New York: The Haworth Press, Inc.

Bratt, P. (2001). Aging, mental health and the faith community. *Journal of Religious Gerontology, 13*, 45-54.

Close, R.E. (2000). Logotherapy and adult major depression: Psychotheological dimensions in diagnosing the disorder. In M.A. Kimble (Ed.), *Viktor Frankl's contribution to spirituality and aging*. New York: The Haworth Press, Inc.

Commonwealth Department of Health and Ageing (2001). *Challenge Depression. A manual to help staff identify and reduce depression in aged care facilities.*

Fleming, R. (2002). Depression and spirituality in Australian aged care homes. *Journal of Religious Gerontology, 13*, 107-116.

Jewell, A. (1999). *Spirituality and Ageing*. London: Jessica Kingsley.

Kimble, M.A. (2001). Beyond the biomedical paradigm: Generating a spiritual vision of ageing. In E. MacKinlay, J.W. Ellor & S. Pickard (Eds.), *Aging, spirituality and pastoral care: A multinational perspective*. New York: The Haworth Pastoral Press.

Kitwood, T. (1997). *Dementia reconsidered: The person comes first*. Buckingham, England: Open University Press.

Koenig, H.G. (2001). Spiritual assessment in medical practice. *American Family Physician, 63*, 30-33.

Koenig, H.G. & Weaver, A.J. (1997a). *Counselling troubled older adults. A handbook for pastors and religious caregivers*. Nashville: Abingdon Press.

Koenig, H.G. & Weaver, A.J. (1997b). *Pastoral care of older adults*. Minneapolis: Fortress Press.

Kubler-Ross, E. (1969). *On death and dying*. New York: Springer.

MacKinlay, E. (2001a). *The Spiritual Dimension of Ageing*. London: Jessica Kingsley.

MacKinlay, E. (2001b). The spiritual dimension of caring: Applying a model for spiritual tasks of ageing. In E. MacKinlay, J.W. Ellor & S. Pickard (Eds.), *Ageing, spirituality and pastoral care: A multinational perspective*. New York: The Haworth Pastoral Press.

McFadden, S. (1995). Religion, spirituality and good old age. *Centre for Aging and Religious Studies*, http://www.luthersem.edu/CARS/newsletters/1995/FALL95.HTM

Moberg, D.O. (1994). *Ageing and God*. New York: The Haworth Press, Inc.

Moberg, D.O. (2001). Research on spirituality. In D.O. Moberg (Ed.), *Aging and Spirituality*. New York: The Haworth Pastoral Press.

Moberg, D.O. (2001a). The Spiritual life review. In D.O. Moberg (Ed.), *Aging and Spirituality*. New York: The Haworth Pastoral Press.

Morgan, R.L. (1996). *Remembering your story: A guide to spiritual autobiography*. Nashville: Upper Room Books.

Mowat, H. & Ryan, D. (2002). Spiritual issues in health and social care: Practice into policy. *Journal of Religious Gerontology, 14*, 51-67.

Rogers, C.R. (1965). *Client-centred therapy: Its current practice, implications and theory*. Boston: Houghton, Mifflin.

Simmons, H.C. and Wilson, J. (2001). *Soulful Ageing*. Macon Georgia: Smyth & Helwys.

Treetops, J. (1999). The memory box. In A. Jewell (Ed.), *Spirituality and Ageing*. London: Jessica Kingsley.

Vaillant, G.E. (2002). *Ageing well*. Melbourne: Scribe Publications.

'Just Because I Can't Remember . . .'
Religiousness in Older People
with Dementia

Corinne Trevitt, RN, MN
Elizabeth MacKinlay, PhD, RN

SUMMARY. This paper reports part of a pilot study that used spiritual reminiscence techniques to explore issues of religiosity, church attendance and meaning in life of a group of older people with dementia. The study used small groups, individual interviews and participant observation to examine the experience of dementia and the search for meaning used by people with dementia. There were 22 participants from three aged care facilities involved in the project. The majority of participants had been long-term church attendees and could describe how their religion and relationship with God had impacted on their lives. They had few fears for the future and derived considerable meaning in life from

Corinne Trevitt is Grad. Dip. Gerontics, Division of Health, Design & Science, School of Health Sciences, Nursing Department University of Canberra, ACT 2601, Australia. Elizabeth MacKinlay is Director, Centre for Ageing and Pastoral Studies, and Associate Professor, School of Theology, Charles Sturt University, 15 Blackall Street, Barton, ACT 2600, Australia (E-mail: emackinlay@csu.edu.au).

The project: "The Search for Meaning: Quality of life for the person with dementia" was made possible through a University of Canberra Collaborative Research Grant with research industry partners Anglican Retirement Community Services and Wesley Gardens Aged Care, 2000-01.

[Haworth co-indexing entry note]: "'Just Because I Can't Remember . . .' Religiousness in Older People with Dementia." Trevitt, Corinne, and Elizabeth MacKinlay. Co-published simultaneously in *Journal of Religious Gerontology* (The Haworth Pastoral Press, an imprint of The Haworth Press, Inc.) Vol. 16, No. 3/4, 2004, pp. 109-121; and: *Spirituality of Later Life: On Humor and Despair* (ed: Rev. Elizabeth MacKinlay) The Haworth Pastoral Press, an imprint of The Haworth Press, Inc., 2004, pp. 109-121. Single or multiple copies of this article are available for a fee from The Haworth Document Delivery Service [1-800-HAWORTH, 9:00 a.m. - 5:00 p.m. (EST). E-mail address: docdelivery@haworthpress.com].

http://www.haworthpress.com/web/JRG
Digital Object Identifier: 10.1300/J078v16n03_08

their relationships with family. Participants were able to describe early memories and also remember things happening recently in their aged care facility. This would seem to be the opposite of community expectations (and sometimes staff expectations) of older people with dementia. *[Article copies available for a fee from The Haworth Document Delivery Service: 1-800-HAWORTH. E-mail address: <docdelivery@haworthpress.com> Website: <http://www. HaworthPress.com> © 2004 by The Haworth Press, Inc. All rights reserved.]*

KEYWORDS. Older people, dementia, religiosity, spirituality, memory, spiritual reminiscence, life meaning

INTRODUCTION

Some assumptions made about people diagnosed with dementia may become barriers to effective communication and well being of these people. Although memory is affected, the ability to enjoy the moment remains intact and remains a powerful force for maintaining dignity and a sense of place for those who can no longer remember recent events. For many people with dementia, recent events have disappeared from their memories as soon as they occur, but older memories remain intact. Some can remember clearly their first day at school but cannot remember what they did yesterday.

Those older memories are an important part of the person and their life meaning, and each person has a unique history of experiences, learning and family; recent memory forms only one aspect of this. Yet assessments of the cognitive status of older people assume an importance that outweighs their significance in the whole of any person's repertoire of being. This can be misleading when decisions of care are based on questions related to cognitive competence, including the day, date and who the government leader is. For older people living in residential care, these questions are at best irrelevant. For them, understanding how they have become the person they are now, and finding meaning in their lives is more important than being able to answer tests of cognitive competence. For the person with dementia, being able to connect with others and to feel nurtured, valued, and that their life has been worthwhile is often far more central to their day-to-day experiences.

This paper will discuss some of the issues raised from a pilot project on spiritual reminiscence work undertaken with older people with a diagnosis of dementia and residing in aged care facilities. In particular, this paper will focus on religiosity and the spiritual dimension of the participants. The participants in this study had experienced rich and varied lives and the majority had participated in organised religion. Most took life as it came, sometimes laughed about their lack of memory and found great comfort and pleasure from their families. They derived considerable pleasure from the interactions with their fellow participants in the small groups during the study.

Background

Dementia is a condition feared by many older people (MacKinlay, 1998). Although generally viewed as being one disease, dementia is in fact the symptom of many different diseases. The course of the disease is dependent on the type of dementia the older person is experiencing. The most common dementia is Alzheimer's disease. When we speak of dementia, most people use the terms dementia and Alzheimer's disease interchangeably. Alzheimer's disease has a specific course or progression beginning with memory lapses, difficulty learning new information and altered attention span to total physical and cognitive decline. The disease may have a course of as little as 18 months up to 27 years, while the average length of the condition is 10-12 years (Davis, 1999). About 60% of people diagnosed with dementia have Alzheimer's disease.

Vascular dementia is the next most common cause of dementia. This type of dementia is caused by small emboli or infarcts affecting the blood supply to different parts of the brain. The types of behaviour seen are directly related to the area of the brain affected. Where Alzheimer's disease is progressive and relatively predictable, the course of dementia caused by vascular problems is characterised by dips and plateaus over time. However, both types of dementia may be present in the one person. Other less common causes of dementia include Pick's disease, Huntington's disease, Parkinson's disease, alcoholism and infections (Miller, 2004). Current management of the condition is complex, with a current focus on maintaining those affected at home for as long as possible. Usually, institutional care is required during the later stages of dementia. Admission to aged care facilities usually occurs as a result of unmanageable behaviour such as aggression, incontinence, or being unable to be left living alone for safety issues.

Commonly held views about dementia assume that the person with dementia is unaware of, and unable to communicate with others. A number of authors challenge this view and describe numerous instances where a person with dementia demonstrates considerable communication skill and insight if only carers were willing to take the time to listen and use alternative communication strategies (Killick article in this collection of essays; Killick & Allen, 2001; McFadden & Hanusa, 1998; Kitwood, 1997; Goldsmith, 1996).

Spiritual reminiscence helps to guide and encourage the search for meaning for older people with or without dementia. This search often seems to become more urgent as people grow older (Erikson, 1986; Frankl, 1984; Kimble, 1995) and become increasingly aware of their own mortality. The search for meaning is common to all humans, although individual response to meaning and the depth of the search varies between individuals. Erikson (1986) described the final stages of psychosocial development as integrity versus despair, and the contrast is often evident among older people, some who exhibit a great sense of peace and joy in their lives, while others show despair. Reminiscence or life review is a naturally occurring event that most people seem to engage in (Butler, 1963; Bornat, 1994; Coleman, 1986, 1994, 1999), and is connected with coming to that sense of integrity in later life. Spiritual reminiscence, and particularly, coming to a sense of final meanings is part of this process (MacKinlay, 2001).

An Exploratory Study of Spiritual Reminiscence Work with People Who Have Dementia

In a collaborative project between the University of Canberra and two industry partners, Anglican Retirement Community Services and Wesley Gardens Aged Care, a new way of connecting with those with dementia was explored using spiritual reminiscence. Spiritual reminiscence work uses techniques to facilitate the search for meaning. While it is often thought that these techniques require good cognitive skills, these techniques can also be used to help the person with dementia deal with past events including resentment, guilt, anger and the need for reconciliation. Spiritual reminiscence may help individuals reframe past events and come to a sense of integrity in their life journey (Kimble, 1995; MacKinlay, 1998, 2001). Spiritual reminiscence work has been identified as a way of helping older people with memory loss find meaning in their lives as they cope with the day-to-day difficulties of memory loss.

This project aimed to explore the use of spiritual reminiscence with people who live with dementia. The project used small groups, individual interviews and participant observation to examine the experience of dementia, the search for meaning and coping strategies used by people with dementia. There were 22 participants from three aged care facilities involved in the project. Prior to the commencement of the small groups, each participant was interviewed about what gives them meaning in their lives now, what they remember about happy and sad times in the past, how they respond to formal and informal spiritual and religious activities, what they look forward to during their remaining years and how carers and family can help them now. The small groups then met weekly for six weeks or for five months and explored these issues in more detail. All interactions were taped and transcribed for analysis. Analysis was assisted by the NUD*IST Qualitative Data Analysis computer package. Ethics permission was gained from the university and each of the study sites for this project.

Memories of Religious Activities and Religion Now in the Lives of Participants

Results from the in depth interviews and weekly group sessions identified much about each participant's interaction with religious activities. The majority had attended church and expressed an ongoing relationship with God. They spoke of early memories of Sunday school attendance and of the community support they had through the church. Many spoke of their ongoing relationship with God and the importance of this to their lives. Participants identified issues that gave the most meaning to their lives and described their hopes for the future.

Earliest Memories of Church

Respondents spoke at length about their early memories of church. For many, their earliest memories came from when they were four or five years old. Their memories were very clear and they described in detail their experiences. One response to earliest memories of church was "My father was an organist and I used to pump the organ for him . . . I was too young to understand where I was, I would be about three or four." Another respondent remembered well back into her childhood, " . . . well I used to go to Sunday school, when we came out from England I was about five and I went to Sunday school here and then the church services." One respondent remembered " . . . Being told to sit still and I could never sit still."

Almost all participants had memories of early church attendance. It was obviously something that was part of usual family life. One participant said "I had to go to church every Sunday, we're Catholic." She goes on to describe going to confession and inventing stories because "I never did anything wrong . . . . it would make it more interesting." Another woman talked about how she stopped going to church following her marriage because " . . . I married a man that was against the church . . . " but she went on to describe how she " . . . never forgot her prayers."

One participant talked about her loss of faith. She had been a regular church attendee and had faith in God but and still felt that faith could help other people. But for her "my husband was ill with arthritis for about nine months, he really suffered and I think I lost my faith . . ."

For a number of respondents the church was an important part of their community and added to the sense of community cohesion. Participants frequently mention how they could catch up with friends while at church. Their experiences also date from a time when going to church was a usual part of family life. One participant said: "I think going to church on a Sunday and being able to meet my friends and that's it I think." Another mentioned how it was a usual part of life "I started going to Sunday school very early in life and church activities, it was the normal way of life. . . ." One participant was keen to ensure that we knew that he did not go to church for the community connection but because of his wish to worship "I did not go just for that . . . "

Another participant talked about how he became more involved in church activities as he grew up. "Yes I did, because all my friends seemed to be there and it was a nice place to go and then we all became bible study teachers and we worked towards that from the first day we went to Sunday school-that was the idea of our being there."

For these people with dementia, early experiences of church included not only the religious rituals, but also a strong sense of community and social connection. As with other community members in their cohort, church was an accepted part of their lives.

Church and Religious Activities Now

Participants still continue to attend the church services in the aged care facility in part to enjoy the social contact that these services provide. In response to the question about their attendance and enjoyment of services in the facility, one respondent says "Yes I do, really, and I enjoy being with people." The need for connection with others was clearly evident in this response.

Some participants expressed how meaning in their lives came through their faith relationship. The following interchange reflects this.

In response to: "What gives you most meaning?" one participant replied "I think my family . . . and being able to go to church on Sunday, and my friends." One woman, a regular church attendee, was asked where she found meaning in her religion and she responded: "Well it makes it the meaning to life." Another said: "Well it's part of living."

One week during the group meeting a participant expressed her frustration and dismay that the service for that week had been cancelled. She felt the lack of ability to participate for a week considerably impacted on her "I hate missing church, I feel like I've let people down." Another respondent expressed her wish to attend Mass. Although the aged care facility had weekly services in the multi-denominational chapel, she missed the peace she gained from being in a Catholic church. Too often, it is thought that people with dementia would not know, or remember whether they went to church, yet the participants in this study were able to articulate their wishes, when they were given an opportunity.

One man said: "I'm Christian but I'm not a devoted person who goes to church just to be seen to go to church. I go to the church to act for what I did, that's it. I think many church goers just want to be seen to have been in the church." There is still a perception that people do go to church 'just to be seen' although it would seem this is very much less the case in Australia in recent decades (Kaldor, 1994).

Relationship with God

The participants had a lot to say about God and their relationship with God. The majority described an ongoing and constant relationship that always helped to sustain them through good and bad times. Participants described how they prayed every day and felt that their prayers were answered. When a participant was asked: "Do you have a sense of how you feel when you think of God?" The response was: "Well I feel he's close to me and we are close together."

In response to a question about their image of God, participants were very descriptive of the role God had played and continued to play in their lives. The majority had a close connection with their God. One participant responded: "Just he's always there, everywhere and you get help." Another replied, "I'm not quite sure, but I hope he's OK." Another response was, "Yes I have my own sort of talk with him." Another woman said: "Oh yes I do believe very much in God if I can say a little prayer I feel he listens to me."

Two participants felt that God had let them down. They were unable to account for why God allows things to happen that are negative or hurtful. One of these participants expressed her sense of God in relation to the death of her husband: "I can't tell you how much, I miss him such, a good man. We did everything together, everything, we'd never go out of our way to do anything for each other I mean just for ourselves it was for each other, I wonder why God destroys you this way."

Another woman remarked: "I have no faith in him (God) at all now, I used to when I was younger but it has all gone, a few things have happened that have upset me and I think, oh well there is no God. I don't know, I just feel as though I am not interested now."

In contrast, another response was: "God, Oh yes he's been with me all my life, he has been with me not me with him. He's been with me, yes I do I appreciate God as a being and he must love me because otherwise I wouldn't be here."

Meaning in Life Amongst the Participants

During all the sessions with this group of participants, by far the most important source of meaning in life was relationship. Family was often not only important in itself, but gave meaning to the person's whole existence. Often when asked "what brings greatest meaning for you?" It was in terms of family, spouse, children, and grandchildren. For those who had no family, there was sadness. "Oh my family have been the most important" typified responses here.

However, another expressed the feelings of those who find later life a burden when she said: "Oh I feel as though I'm over meaning." One woman said she had difficulties in finding meaning since she has developed cataracts. She is also deaf. She still says however that the important things in life for her now are: "My relations, my daughters are everything to me."

For still others, a sense of the importance of environment remains with them. Walking provides pleasure for some, while reading is important for others. Gardening was also still of interest to some, although they were often unable to participate.

For one participant when asked: "What makes life worthwhile for you now?" She replied: "I like being alive!" Another said: "Living, I suppose." "Living, I should think, I mean I enjoy my life here. I've made lots of friends here." So life was still worth living, even though this person was living with dementia and was a resident in an aged care facility, which by definition meant that she was unable to live by herself in the community, having been assessed for need of residential aged care.

Dementia and Life Meaning: Discussion of the Study Findings

When reading the transcripts from this study, it is often easy to forget that all the participants in this study have a medical diagnosis of dementia. They are all affected to the extent that they can no longer live on their own and make their decisions. This paper has only reported material from the transcriptions of this study, of the themes of religious practice, and spirituality, and has touched briefly on life meaning for these people. However, it can readily be seen that participants were able to describe early memories and also remember things happening in their aged care facility. This would seem to be the opposite of the community expectations (and sometimes staff expectations) of older people with dementia.

For the majority of participants, the church had formed a significant part of their earlier lives and it continued to be important as they aged. They valued church as a community as well as to enhance their relationship with God. They grew up in a time in Australia when church attendance was usual for families. There has been a gradual decline in church attendance in Australia from the 1950s. In 1950, 45% of the population declared they went regularly to church, by 2000 this had decreased to 20% (Bellamy, Black, Castle, Hughes & Kaldor, 2002). In a discussion with Malcolm Goldsmith (pers. com. 2000) he wondered how we could reach people in the future who have dementia. He described situations where, by singing a well-known hymn, he could get people to sing along and begin to interact. What will become the memory trigger when these old hymns are no longer well known?

Almost all the participants described clearly their image of God. Even the participants who had lost their faith still had a picture of God. Many participants actively prayed to God each day and had an image of a friend, a strong person, or a powerful person, with whom they had an ongoing relationship. One participant talked of how she missed going to a Catholic Church and experiencing a Mass. Others missed the church services when they were cancelled at the last minute. Goldsmith (2001) discusses the role of ritual in people with dementia. Being able to attend church and participate in a familiar ritual can help to reinforce the sense of identity and community that is often missing in an older person with dementia. He describes how ritual can empower but also trap-identifying the correct rituals is important.

Discussion of issues concerned with religion and spirituality rarely occurs within an aged care facility. There are a number of reasons for this including lack of time on the part of the staff, the feeling that this is the role of the pastoral carer rather than the care staff and that staff may be embarrassed by asking these 'touchy' questions. It is obviously easier to discuss the action of bowels rather than meaning in life. David Snowden describes an amusing incident when an elderly man with dementia, who had almost ceased to speak to his wife, was very talkative when asked about his 'feelings' in a study interview. Imagine his wife's surprise when she suddenly heard her husband's voice from the other room. One of the things he said to Danner (researcher): 'I don't talk anymore because no-one listens anymore' (Snowden, 2001, p. 195). Killick and Allan (2001) describe the importance of communication skills when interacting with those with dementia. Issues such as knowledge of the person's life story, listening and not interrupting, taking risks and asking questions we might not feel comfortable about are all important when communicating with this group of older people.

In this study, meaning was almost synonymous with relationship. The need for relationship seemed stronger than with previously studied groups of people who did not have dementia (MacKinlay, 2001a, 2001b). There was more material on relationship contained within the interviews and group sessions in this study than on any other single topic. Many of these people talked much about family, recalling various incidents around family events. Some became confused about exact relationships, and whether the children were theirs, or perhaps the children some spoke of were their grandchildren. It is necessary to move beyond the confusion of words to seek meaning in what these people are saying. Often relatives will say: "She does not know me" What does this really mean? Although the person with dementia may get the names or generations incorrect, the underlying meaning for themselves remains the family and those relationships. There is a sense, that as Boden wrote (1998) that the name may be forgotten, but she still would 'know' who the person was. She was using 'knowing' is a different way. It was suggested that this was a 'label' effect, perhaps as a computer file may be lost. It's probably still there somewhere, but may be difficult to open.

The need for emotional intimacy does not seem to diminish in later life, whether or not the person has dementia. When dementia is part of the scene it complicates relationship patterns. The communication problems that occur are hard to deal with at times. However, it does not mean that these people don't want relationship; on the contrary, the need for relationship seems undiminished. Kitwood's psychological needs of people with dementia clearly illustrates this. He lists these needs as centred on the need for love, and to include attachment, identity, comfort, occupation and inclusion (Kitwood, 1997). Several of the women in this study spoke of their desire for relationship with a man. One woman talked of going dancing and said: "I'll never marry again just want friendship."

One of the issues explored in the groups was related to participants' fears for the future. All participants responded that they had no fears and that as long as they were healthy they had nothing to worry about. In a similar study with cognitively intact older people nearly all participants expressed a fear of dementia or of 'being off my legs and out of my mind' (MacKinlay, 2001a). It is interesting to note that in the group with dementia, the fear of losing your mind was no longer evident and although they would occasionally joke about poor memory, this was not an overriding concern.

These responses from the in-depth interviews and weekly small group sessions showed that these nursing home residents with dementia felt free to talk about religion and what it meant to them, both individually and within the groups. Both positive and negative images of God were shared and it was possible to support and affirm participants as appropriate. Yet sometimes staff in aged care facilities feel uncomfortable in speaking about religious and spiritual issues with residents. Therefore, it must be asked, if the topic is of importance to residents, then surely staff should be able to support these people in the practice of their religion, whether or not the staff hold similar beliefs themselves. This is not of course to suggest that all staff should become providers of spiritual care. However, a basic understanding and willingness to learn of resident religious and spiritual needs is essential. It is noted though that some aspects of spiritual and religious care are specifically within the roles of chaplains and pastoral workers. One of the participants at the end of one of the group sessions concluded by saying "thank you for this talk; it is not often we are able to talk about these things."

CONCLUSION

The process of this study provided valuable information on communication with older people who have dementia. Analysis of the transcripts showed that, given the possibility of someone to listen to them, and provide time for communication in a supporting environment enables these people with dementia to share their beliefs and life meaning, sometimes in quite deep ways. This chapter has focused on only a small area of the rich data obtained during the study on religious activities and beliefs, spirituality and meaning in life.

Findings clearly demonstrated the importance of religious activities for these people, the images they held of God and past memories of church combined with their present religious activities. These activities provide both for their relationship with God and for a sense of community, being with other people. It is noted that some in the study did not participate in religious activities at all but they still were active and voluntary participants in the groups, apparently comfortable sharing the lack of religious belief. The sense of spiritual seemed to bridge the gap between those for whom religious practices were important and those for whom they were not important.

REFERENCES

Bellamy, J. Black, A. Castle, K., Hughes & Kaldor, P. (2002). *Why people don't go to Church.* Sydney: NCLS.

Boden, C. (1998). *Who will I be when I die?* Melbourne: Harper Collins Religious.

Bornat, J. (ed) (1994). *Reminiscence Reviewed.* Buckingham: Open University Press.

Butler, R. N. (1963). 'The Life Review: An Interpretation of Reminiscence in the Aged.' In Neugarten, B. L. (ed.) (1968), *Middle Age and Aging: A Reader in Social Psychology.* Chicago: The University of Chicago Press.

Coleman, P. G. (1986). *Ageing and Reminiscence Processes: Social and Clinical Implications.* Chichester: John Wiley & Sons.

Coleman, P. G. (1994). 'Reminiscence within the study of ageing: The social significance of story.' In J. Bornat, (Ed.), *Reminiscence Reviewed.* Buckingham: Open University Press.

Coleman, P.G. (1999). Creating a life story: The task of reconciliation. *The Gerontologist,* 39(2), 133-139.

Davis, H. (1999). Delirium & Dementia. In Stone, J. Wyman, J. & Salisbury, S., *Clinical Gerontological Nursing.* Philadelphia: W.B. Saunders.

Goldsmith, M. (1996). *Hearing the voice of people with dementia: Opportunities and obstacles.* London: Jessica Kingsley Publishers.

Goldsmith, M. (2001). When words are no longer necessary: A gift of ritual. In MacKinlay, E., Ellor, J. & Pickard, S. (eds.), *Aging, Spirituality and Pastoral Care.* New York: The Haworth Pastoral Press.

Killick, J. & Allan, K. (2001). *Communication and the care of people with dementia.* Buckingham: Open University Press.

Kimble, M. A, McFadden S. H, Ellor, J. W, & Seeber, J. J. (eds) (1995). *Ageing, Spirituality and Religion: A Handbook.* Minneapolis: Augsburg Fortress Press.

MacKinlay, E.B. (2001a). *The Spiritual Dimension of Ageing.* London: Jessica Kingsley.

MacKinlay E. B. (2001b). Health, healing and wholeness in frail elderly people. *Journal of Religious Gerontology*. 13 (2), 25-34.

Miller, C. (2004). *Nursing for Wellness in Older Adults*. Lippincott, Philadelphia: Wilkins & Williams.

Snowdon, D. (2001). *Aging with Grace*. New York: Bantam Books.

Stone, J. Wyman, J. & Salisbury, S. (1999). *Clinical Gerontological Nursing*. Philadelphia: W.B. Saunders.

Hope Rising Out of Despair: The Spiritual Journey of Patients Admitted to a Hospice

Ann Harrington, PhD, RN

SUMMARY. It is noted that the suddenness of grief and loss awakens individuals to their own spiritual journey. Studies have shown that spirituality increases when death is faced (Derrickson 1996; Millison & Dudley 1992) with others indicating the need for those living with dying patients, to be in touch with their own spirituality (English 1998; Irion 1988). This paper, part of a larger PhD study, reports conversations with patients as to their spiritual 'journey.' Their responses were categorised using a three step framework generated by Chandler (1999) which incorporates elements of grief from Perlman, and Takaacs (1990). Their responses give some indication as to their level of 'despair' and 'hope' whilst on their spiritual journey and gives health care providers guidance as to how to assist patients with their spiritual needs. *[Article copies available for a fee from The Haworth Document Delivery Service: 1-800-HAWORTH. E-mail address: <docdelivery@haworthpress.com> Website: <http://www.HaworthPress.com> © 2004 by The Haworth Press, Inc. All rights reserved.]*

Ann Harrington is Senior Lecturer, School of Nursing and Midwifery, Flinders University, Adelaide, South Australia.

This work was completed as part of a larger PhD thesis from the School of Nursing and Midwifery, Flinders University, South Australia, Australia.

[Haworth co-indexing entry note]: "Hope Rising Out of Despair: The Spiritual Journey of Patients Admitted to a Hospice." Harrington, Ann. Co-published simultaneously in *Journal of Religious Gerontology* (The Haworth Pastoral Press, an imprint of The Haworth Press, Inc.) Vol. 16, No. 3/4, 2004, pp. 123-145; and: *Spirituality of Later Life: On Humor and Despair* (ed: Rev. Elizabeth MacKinlay) The Haworth Pastoral Press, an imprint of The Haworth Press, Inc., 2004, pp. 123-145. Single or multiple copies of this article are available for a fee from The Haworth Document Delivery Service [1-800-HAWORTH, 9:00 a.m. - 5:00 p.m. (EST). E-mail address: docdelivery@haworthpress.com].

http://www.haworthpress.com/web/JRG
© 2004 by The Haworth Press, Inc. All rights reserved.
Digital Object Identifier: 10.1300/J078v16n03_09

KEYWORDS. Spiritual journey, spirituality, palliative care, hospice

INTRODUCTION

Studies identify that a propensity toward spirituality increases when death is faced (Derrickson 1996; Millison & Dudley 1992) and that dying can push us from the superficial into the deep very quickly (English 1998). As we face our own death or that of a loved one, a spiritual journey begins.

Pryor (1989) chronicles some of the classics in spiritual journeying from a Christian perspective. Citing early beginnings as pre-AD 1100 with Augustine of Hippo (354-430AD) and post-AD 1100, including such seminal texts as John Bunyan's *The Pilgrim's Progress*, Martin Luther (1483-1546) and John Wesley (1703-1791), her bibliography continues to the 20th century, including Thomas Merton, Rudolf Otto and Smith Wigglesworth.

When it comes to spiritual growth within the 20th Century, James Fowler is one of the most widely read on 'stages' of development. His 1981 publication used theories of human development from Piaget, Erikson and Kohlberg, proffering six stages under his rubric of 'faith.' His publication was a beginning framework for Scott Peck (1987) who wrote of spiritual 'growth.' Peck (1987) claims that although Fowler offers six stages, he has restricted his work to four, and, despite some overlap, there is no contradiction.

As this was a qualitative study seeking only a simple comparison, Fowler (1981) and Peck's (1987) theories were all considered rather lengthy for the purpose of this exercise. Consequently an author was chosen using a nursing perspective and with a Christian orientation. Chandler (1999) writes of 'spiritual journeys' that 'involve us in the mystery of experiencing the holy' (1999, p. 64) and her framework was used to 'plot' the spiritual journeys of patients within this study. As her framework consists of only three stages, its simplicity affords good opportunity to determine where individuals might be placed along a continuum of spiritual development.

Chandler (1999) uses Joseph Campbell's (1968) argument (although he wrote of mythical journeys) where he suggests the standard path of the hero in a journey is 'a magnification of the formal, represented in the rites of passage: separation-initiation-return.' Incorporating Campbell's (1968) framework and adding Perlman and Takacs' (1990) elements of grief, Chandler (1999) argues that stories of 'transformation' along a journey are usually made up of three distinct stages. Likening this journey to a three act play, she claims there is a beginning, middle and an end. The phases of the journey leading us from the old to the new can be described as incorporating grief, denial, anger, bargaining, chaos, depression, resignation, openness, readiness and re-emergence Chandler (1999) collapses these 10 into a three-fold process (Table 1).

TABLE 1

1.	loss of structure	([grief] denial, anger, bargaining)
2.	chaos: into the woods	(chaos, depression, resignation)
3.	re-structuring	(openness, readiness, re-emergence)

It should be remembered however, that patients diagnosed with a terminal illness face overwhelming change in their lives. They must contend not only with the progression of their disease, but also with personal and professional losses. Redding (2000) cites these losses as: loss of relationships, personal identity, physical abilities, sexual capacity, self-care and a potential future (2000, p. 205). Nonetheless, research has indicated patients are better equipped to deal with loss and change if they have developed spiritually (Fleming 2001; Moberg 2001; Thoresen 1999).

When news of terminal illness is given to patients and/or their relatives, no-one remains unaffected. Moving from a state of denial to acceptance and back again, whilst trying to deal with such adverse news is commonplace. Our Western view of health and the biomedical model's insistence on 'cure at all costs' (often suggesting a failure on the part of the health care provider if patients are not 'cured') only frustrates our attempts to deal with death and dying issues. Indeed Koestenbaum (1976) argues that in the western world, the subject of death 'is locked in a closet or tucked away in a dark corner' (1976, p. 1). Balk (1999) suggests that once bereavement can be embraced, our assumptions can be challenged and this can provide some grounds for spiritual change.

Within this study patients' opinions were sought regarding their spiritual needs and their responses were 'plotted' on Chandler's (1999) Table 1. To begin the discussion questions were framed around issues of meaning. For example questions asked 'what gives you strength, what gives you hope, what gives meaning to your life?' As a result the following excerpts from transcripts captures the view of four patients who consented to interview.

Erica

> I think it must have been about 30 years ago, I had a little tiny cyst on my ear . . . and I showed it to my doctor and he said it's a sebaceous cyst so he had it x-rayed and showed on the x-ray a little cyst. So nothing was done about it and it didn't worry me. . . . (. . .) And then it did enlarge a little so I went back to him . . . Well it was very hot weather . . . (. . .) and I was supposed to go and have a biopsy and a scan. Well I let it go for 18 months. But whether that would have made any difference, I think it was established by then. I was sure of it . . .

Spirituality for Erica

Erica had attended a church school during her youth. Now at 84, her church and her previous schooling were held in high esteem:

> Researcher: What's been the most influential people or the most influential things that happened in your life. In your past?

> Erica: Oh dear. I can't really . . . I can't put my finger on anything really. I enjoyed my life. My school life and my sporting life . . . (. . .). I went to a Church of England school. We were brought up in a good Church . . . (. . .). I'm just a church goer and love my church and believe . . .

For Erica, although her spirituality included church attendance and contained a God dimension and prayer, it was a private matter:

> Erica: I mean if I want them they'll come and see me. And they ring me up and have talks but I don't want to let it be known all through the church. I want to live my own quiet life . . . (. . .) Several people pray for me. And that's how I want it. I don't want it advertised.

> Researcher: . . . and what's the role of religion in your illness? Has that had any effect at all?

> Erica: Not really. I talk to God a lot . . . when I go to bed at night.

When it came to the spiritual domain, consistent with her desire for privacy Erica declined any specific help in this area. Yet given her church background, I inquired regarding spiritual care:

> Researcher: Is it all right for me to talk to you about spiritual things? You feel comfortable about that?
>
> Erica: Oh yes.
>
> Researcher: You haven't had anybody from the pastoral care team you've needed to talk to at all?
>
> Erica: Not really.

Erica was content to 'let things roll along' and did not wish to speak about death or dying:

> Erica: I don't want to know when I'm going to die. I'm just taking life as it comes . . . I don't want to say when it will be or that sort of thing I'm just going along with it.
>
> Researcher: (. . .) And what is giving you hope at the moment?
>
> Erica: Well, I am a believer. I'm not that religious but I'm Church of England and I just hope. Well I don't think there is much hope. I mean it's just got to go its course. So I don't sit and think about it very much.

Although Erica was happy to speak to me about spiritual caring, she declined any specific assistance in the area. In common with her need for privacy, she did not wish to elaborate on any needs in the spiritual domain:

> Researcher: Since we are talking about spiritual care here, what sort of spiritual care would you like to see . . . (. . .) would there be anything that the nurses could do in that area?
>
> Erica: Not really. Not at the moment. I don't know what's ahead of me.

She preferred not to think about the future. Her closing remarks typified this view:

> Researcher: Well thank you very much for talking to me. It's very kind of you.
>
> Erica: It's a pleasure. I never thought this sort of thing would happen to me. But you don't do you? You go along in life and enjoy it and never think of the consequences.

Discussion of Erica's Interview

Erica's condition had begun some 30 years ago. At that time she had chosen not to pursue aggressively any treatment.

Her spirituality included a God dimension and her church, which she loved. She spoke to God 'a lot' through prayer nightly, although her need for privacy meant she did not wish anyone to pray with her in the hospice setting, nor out loud in church. When it came to spiritual care, although several people prayed for her, she 'didn't want it advertised.'

Chandler's Framework

In spite of her age (84 years), according to Chandler's (1999) schema Erica could be said to be at the beginning of her spiritual journey. This beginning phase-*loss of structure*-includes the elements of *denial, anger and bargaining*. Although when I spoke to her there was no apparent anger or bargaining, it appeared Erica had lived for many years in what Chandler (1999) would term 'denial.' Even though Erica's illness began about 30 years ago, it did not concern her so she chose not to do anything about it. Despite the fact her growth increased in size, she avoided both a biopsy and a scan because of the hot weather. This increase in size did not provoke Erica sufficiently for her to seek treatment and there was a reluctance on her part to attend to the possibility of her condition progressing to its terminal stage.

Chandler (1999) (Table 1) writes that 'shaking of our foundations' in the early stages of a difficult diagnosis means it is often easier to avoid dealing with adverse news. Erica had lived her life with some stability and she was relatively young (54 years old) when her cyst first appeared. It would have been easier to ignore any sinister implications of her growth. There is the possibility of course, at this stage, that removal of the cyst could have cured her. That was not Erica's view when I spoke to her. 'I think it was established by then,' she stated. Perhaps this belief gave her some solace in her later years, finding it had progressed to the terminal stage.

Chandler (1999) suggests if we can overcome denial in these beginning stages, then the impact of the losses associated with the diagnosis becomes apparent. The need to acknowledge these negative feelings enables the individual to move into the next phase of the journey. Chandler (1999) comments that it is critically important to be able to sit with 'the emptiness, the pain of loneliness, separation anxiety, confusion and bewilderment' (1999, p. 65). Failure to attend to these feelings by avoiding the pain of transition may leave us unable to move on:

> ... as this first juncture sets the stage for a trajectory of avoidance as a method of coping that can begin to take on a life of its own ... and can truncate the spiritual journey from the beginning. (1999, p. 65)

Chandler (1999) believes hope can be found even in this despairing period:

> It's much easier to tolerate the aching absence of feeling if there is a viable alternative offering hope. Hope in this context implies ... that some phoenix will indeed rise up from these ashes of sadness, frustration and disappointment. (Chandler 1999, p. 65)

This is where issues of spirituality can be relevant. Erica's words, 'I don't think there is much hope,' identified that she acknowledged the fact that her condition was terminal (possibly giving up hoping for hope), and although she indicated she was not ready to think about it then, it may have been embraced later.

Erica's final comments to me indicated some re-evaluation of her life: 'you never think of the consequences,' and 'I never thought this sort of thing would happen to me. But you don't do you?' Her reflective mood indicates she may well have considered some of the consequences. Although she did not want to discuss spiritual issues then ('not at the moment'), her imminent discharge from the hospice indicated she would be readmitted at some stage and she may then be at a different place spiritually.

These closing remarks serve to reinforce studies which found that illness, particularly terminal illness, activates a spiritual quest (Kuuppelomaki 2001; Derrickson 1996; Millison & Dudley 1992; Harrington 1993). Thirty years ago when Erica had been first diagnosed with a potential malignancy, her need for spiritual care was not a priority. It did, however, stimulate her thinking in this area. Although spiritual issues were private for Erica, and she did not express any spiritual need, for her such assistance may be just sitting with her as she speaks of her loss, or assisting her to get in touch with those thoughts and emotions. The ability to determine where Erica is on her spiritual pathway is the first step in assisting her to find some hope in her situation.

Stan

Stan's reasons for hospitalisation at that time centred around his pain (arising from prostate cancer) and confusion with his medications. At 76 years of age Stan had lived with his condition for some time:

> Stan: I have cancer, bone cancer. Which came after prostate cancer. And I have been in and out of hospital a few times because the pain was so great. They thought it was wise to bring me in to calm me down and get my medicine in order. To make sure I was taking them at the right time and the right medicine. . . . (. . .) they thought that I may have had an infection of some sort . . . And they couldn't have chosen a better hospital. Because the last time I came in it was under almost identical conditions and within 24 hours I was feeling a lot better, in fact back on my feet again.

> Stan: But as soon as I walked in . . . but I didn't walk in I was carried in . . . soon as I came into the hospital . . . I felt much better. (. . .) I felt the peace and tranquillity of the place . . .

He went on to discuss the setting and nursing care, and contrary to Erica, he was keen to speak of spirituality, which for him centred around his faith in God:

> Stan: When I came in here, not having help of Christian faith in the home, coming into [here] helped me to get everything in perspective. You would feel the care and attention emanating from the surrounds of the church. People as well as bricks and mortar . . . (. . .)

> Researcher: And when you say . . . (. . .) when you came in here you felt the peace . . . (. . .) what do you attribute the peace in here to?

Stan: Well I think mainly it's the feeling I got was, the people in here, I don't know whether they are hand picked or not, but people like 'Lois' and 'Rachel' and the others, they are dedicated to their job and everything emanates from them.

Spirituality for Stan

Stan: was very open about having 'faith in the Lord.' When I asked him to clarify the 'Lord' and how he had maintained hope throughout the period of his illness, he replied:

> Stan: Oh hope. I have a strong feeling of faith of the Lord. And some people might poo poo it but I don't because it's given me hope and given me strength to rely on. Even my family they know that I'm this way inclined they don't laugh out right at me but I know darn well they've got doubts. But I've got no doubts. It gives me strength and that's all I'm worried about.

> Researcher: Right. So when you talk about the Lord . . . do you mean the Lord Jesus Christ?

> Stan: Yes, of course I do.

Unlike Erica, the church did not mean as much to him but he was clear that he was a Christian:

> Stan: I call myself a Christian although I'm not a church going Christian. I know I have the [Holy] Spirit there but . . . no one can take my faith away from me. It gives me such a strength.

For Stan, an important part of his life was the role of prayer:

> Researcher: Have you got a lot of strength from the Lord at this time while you've had your cancer?

> Stan: Oh yeah . . . it's the strength that . . . it's there. I wake up 2 or 3 o'clock in the morning and I say my prayers and sometimes I can sit there for half an hour or three quarters of an hour and just sit there and think and say my prayers and I get a wonderful feeling of having someone with me in the room. (. . .)Yeah . . . it's just something there. It calms me down and gives me peace.

I asked him about the role of religion in his life:

> Researcher: And . . . so would you say that religion has been help-
> ful to you now?

> Stan: My faith has helped me. Faith in the Lord Jesus Christ.

> Researcher: So it's more of a relationship than a religion?

> Stan: Yes, I believe so yeah.

Except for the issue of prayer (in addition to his comments related
above, he had stated . . . I'm willing to accept prayer) he did not elaborate when it came to any other care that might been deemed 'spiritual.'
To clarify this with him, I inquired:

> Researcher: And was there anything else we might be able to help
> you with your spiritual domain? Anything specific?

> Stan: I can't say anything specific. I've had different denomina-
> tions come around and speak to me and they are all willing to come
> back again.

He enjoyed talking about his faith, even to the point of encouraging me
to follow him up at home if I needed to continue the discussion:

> Stan: Well you can always come back. You can always give me a
> ring at home or whatever.

Discussion of Stan's Interview

The trajectory of Stan's disease meant he had been in and out of the
hospice on several occasions. On two of those occasions (his present
and previous admission), this setting assisted him to feel better within
24 hours, enabling him to 'get back on his feet.' Away from his family
he was able to feel what he deemed to be the 'tranquillity' of the setting
and feeling supported in his faith. He was of the opinion that this hospice gave him room to get issues into 'perspective.' Further, it served to
'calm him down,' as he trusted the nursing staff. He believed they were
'hand picked' and dedicated, and intimated that spirituality, 'every-

thing' emanated from them. His is a view consistent with the belief of the pervasiveness of spirituality (Harris 1998).

The spiritual discomfort at home appeared to come from what he perceived as ridicule by his family. Although they did not 'laugh' out loud at him, he believed they had their doubts about the legitimacy of his faith. Despite these doubts and the fact that some people (presumably his family) 'poo poo'ed' his beliefs spiritually, Stan held a firm Christian belief in God. He claimed to 'know' he had the [Holy] 'spirit there,' and stated that this belief gave him 'hope and strength to rely on,' and provided the means for him to live with his illness for the past seven years.

Chandler's Framework

When I met Stan he was not demonstrating any denial, anger, bargaining, chaos, or depression. His conversation identified that he had, in Chandler's terms, moved to stage three, and appeared accepting with an 'openness' to discussion regarding his situation.

He was able to articulate his spiritual way of life quite openly, even to the point of his belief that the hospice's Christian ethos (which was in parallel with his own) was contributing to his peace. He believed his peace in the setting came from both the nursing staff and the hospice ('I couldn't have picked a better one'), appearing to be in contrast to the ridicule of his faith at home ('not having help of Christian faith in the home'). Although he did not elaborate further regarding his difficulties at home, it clearly impacted on his state of mind and his spirituality. The frequent visits to the hospice afforded him a sense of tranquillity and peace, where he was able to pray ('self-prayer,' stage three, Chandler 1999, p. 68).

Prayer was important to him and although he was 'willing to accept prayer' from others, he derived much strength from his own prayer life. He believed while he was praying he had the feeling of someone with him in the room. He attributed his faith to a personal 'relationship' with his Lord (the Lord Jesus Christ of the Christian church), however, he was not at present a member of a church. Nor did he align his spirituality with religion. This faith helped him during the course of his illness. In fact his faith was 'unshaken' and 'still there' despite his terminal condition. Chandler (1999, p. 68) confirms the importance of prayer for those with terminal illness, citing a study by Eisenberg, Davis, Eltner, Appel, Wilkey, Van Rompay and Kessler (1998) that showed a marked increase in the patient's desire for prayer; from 25% in 1990 to 35% in 1997. Against these findings, however, Koenig, McCullough, and Larson (2001) report a 1995 study in the United States that found 90% of people prayed. They confirm this was 'often several times per day' (2001, p. 4).

Stan was open about both his condition and his spiritual journey. He accepted the terminal state of his illness, reminding me (by his reference to his on-going periods of hospitalisation) of this becoming part of his lifestyle. He expressed an overt sense of hope, attributing it to his 'faith in the Lord,' indicating he had found that place in Chandler's terms of re-structuring his life. This openness, readiness and re-emergence (the components of re-structuring) from a spiritual perspective allowed him to admit freely to a personal prayer life, which in turn translated itself into a sense of peace in the midst of his pain.

Knowing of my own Christian faith, Stan seemed keen for me to maintain contact. As I was leaving his room he reminded me that I could always return for further discussion and offered his telephone number at home. I sensed he was someone who desired 'fellowship' with people who had a similar spirituality. Although I did not follow up this contact outside of his admission to the hospice, I recognised Stan's desire to meet with those of a similar spirit. This is in common with what Thomas Moore states when he claims 'the soul [read spirit] is always searching for itself' (1992, p. 198) and when the Christian Bible writes of refreshing our own spirit by not giving up 'meeting together' (Heb.10:25a). Given his spiritual difficulties at home and not currently being an active church member (not gathering with people of a similar spirit on a regular basis), his admission to the hospice served him in a 'church' like way. It provided the spiritual connection he desired at this time in his life.

Joseph

Joseph's entry into the hospice followed several periods of mis-diagnosis with a prior admission to a psychiatric hospital. When his aggressive form of bowel cancer was finally diagnosed, he was transferred to the hospice. At 50 years of age and despite these set backs, his conversation demonstrated an acceptance of his condition:

> Joseph: And my condition is of a serious nature and . . . but I'm not down I'm not depressed, in terms of 'will I live, will I die.' I mean all those questions went through . . . it did, I thought I would be

dead within a couple of weeks. It's good for me to talk to you about this Ann . . .

He expressed his sadness at the losses he experienced, since becoming ill:

> Joseph: It [his illness] had a major impact on my work, very sadly so, because I wanted to work for another five years and it seems that I will not be able to go back to work which will impede me financially as well as my professional development . . . (. . .) I know we shouldn't be preoccupied with possessions and all that sort of thing, however, I've got a new, refurbished beautiful home unit that I've just had painted, a new carpet, new light fittings, new furniture . . .

I inquired as to how he felt about the hospice setting:

> Joseph: I'm very happy here . . . (. . .) I was born in a [church] institution and I might pass away in one, who knows . . . It's been very, very comfortable in this institution.

Spirituality for Joseph

During our conversation I asked him for his views on spirituality. He claimed that his illness had activated a spiritual quest:

> Researcher: You said you'd like to talk a bit more about the spiritual dimension. So how do you see that then in your own life?

> Joseph: It's a very difficult dimension I suppose, isn't it really? . . . (. . .) For me the spiritual dimension is intricately linked with those other . . . the emotional, the physical, all of those sorts of things that go to make up me as a person as I am . . . (. . .) I seem to be leaning more to the spiritual domain as I get older perhaps and not as well as I was when I was young . . . (. . .) I would ask the priest to come and see me each week. I'd ask him to anoint me. Things which outside of this context would never have entered my mind. I would go to work, I would do my job, that would be all there would be to it . . . Mary my partner is Catholic, I go to mass sometimes and I've met with the Protestant . . . (. . .)we're totally ecumenical.

I wondered in pursuing his spiritual quest, whether that included a God dimension. I put to him, the question of hope and his response was a follows:

> Joseph: What is giving me hope is my zest for life, my love for my partner my sister and my family, and my friends. And also, I believe I have a spiritual conviction of faith, be it formalised in a particular religion or not, I'm not quite sure at this stage, but there is something there, greater and stronger than us . . .

> Researcher: And when you say 'a spiritual conviction of faith, be it formalised in a particular religion' would you have a belief in a God?

> Joseph: Yes, very much so, very much so. I was brought up in what was called Methodism, many, many years ago in the country. It was just a very orthodox conventional church . . . (. . .) it gave me a moral framework in which to live my life. It gave me . . . it supported me to develop a system of fundamental values and beliefs . . . (. . .)

> Researcher: Yes, so it's set within the framework of Christianity?

> Joseph: It's not Buddhism or Shintoism or any other particular doctrine. No it's very much a Christian thing.

> Researcher: And does that give you any strength, that dimension?

> Joseph: Yes, I think it would, definitely, yes.

Regarding his spiritual needs:

> Researcher: Is there anything around here that we could do to help you more in the spiritual domain?

> Joseph: Well I'm getting the priest/father person comes in every Tuesday and he prays with me and I like that. I'm not sure of the role of the chaplains whether there's more of an overseeing role. I don't feel well enough to go to the services on Sunday yet . . . (. . .) One of the priests popped in last night just to say 'how are you?' so I like to know that that spiritual thing is there working . . . (. . .).

He was keen to talk to me, and, like Stan, was happy for me to return if I needed to clarify any issues:

Researcher: Is there anything else you wanted to say?

Joseph: No, no. But if you have any other questions be they wider or deeper or more superficial, I'm happy to answer them anytime.

Discussion of Joseph's Interview

I glimpsed Joseph's sadness as he identified the losses he was experiencing. Loss of his ability to work and to live in his home unit. Even though his illness took some time to diagnose (and his admission to a psychiatric hospital prior to diagnosis!), he claimed he was not down or depressed, with hope at this time coming from his ability to maintain his 'zest for life' in spite of this sadness.

This hope remained because of his love for his partner, sister, family and friends, together with his 'spiritual conviction of faith.' He related that at this stage he was not quite sure of his faith, indicating he had been thinking about it, particularly as he believed in 'something there, greater and stronger than us.'

Spiritual caring for Joseph involved visits from the clergy, which meant for him getting 'that spiritual thing . . . working.' He believed his church background of Methodism gave him a moral framework for his life and supported him in his development with a set of 'fundamental values and beliefs.'

Chandler's Framework

Joseph's accepting attitude prompted me to ask whether his strength was derived from his spiritual convictions. However, unlike Stan, Joseph was somewhat hesitant when I asked him whether this gave him strength. 'I think it would, definitely, yes,' reflecting that his illness had caused him to consider these issues, although at this stage he was not sure. However, he did not appear to be depressed or chaotic in his thinking. In Chandler's (1999) terms, Joseph was in stage two, moving towards stage three of his spiritual quest. Despite the losses he was experiencing this had not impacted on him to the point of depression although initially he thought he would be dead 'within a couple of weeks.' Now he had a measure of hope in that no-one knew how long he had. 'I was born in a [church] institution and I might die in one. Who knows?'

Interestingly, he acknowledged that although spirituality had 'a very difficult dimension,' he appeared to have recognised its holistic nature, linking it with both the emotional and the physical, in his words 'those sorts of things that go to make me up as a person . . .' These comments seem to align his view to what has been stated previously here as the 'pervasiveness of spirituality.'

Getting older, he claimed to be 'leaning more to the spiritual domain . . . ,' although in valuing his quest now, it was 'not as well' as when he was young. Proffering a difference between his youth and now, in his early years he would ask a priest to see him each week, whereas in his later years, prior to his illness, he had not requested the services of a priest. However, now in his illness he was again requesting those services.

Joseph's spirituality was different from Stan's (who spoke of a close 'relationship' with God and a tendency to pray on his own at night). Joseph's spirituality (at least his prayer life) may have been somewhat remote, requiring the assistance of the clergy to reach his God. When I prompted him regarding a belief in God, he responded, 'Yes, very much so, very much so,' although at this stage of his illness he preferred to have the 'priest/father person' come in every Tuesday to assist him with his prayer life.

In discussing his spiritual awakening in his later life, Joseph noted that as he matured, unlike in his youth, he would now have the priest anoint him, which 'outside of this context [this practice] would never have entered' his mind. Previously, he would go to work and do his job and 'that would be all there would be to it.' However, now this spiritual journey had led him to a Christian faith, which was a combination of his previous 'Methodist' upbringing and Roman Catholic Mass with his partner. He claimed this allowed he and his partner to be 'totally ecumenical.'

Chandler (1999) writes of the sensory component of spiritual care. Using the senses via symbols (prayer, music, art, candles, etc.) can afford patients an opportunity to express themselves and 'discover or un-cover their deepest spiritual yearnings' (1999, p. 71). Prayer for Joseph was an important emerging symbol. Further, for those patients who have not progressed to stage three and in some way still may be carrying their burden of pain, we need, 'as people committed to spiritual care . . . to create sacred space for patients' (Chandler 1999, p. 71). In other words, we invite patients to share their stories by providing a way for them to displace their burden. My conversation with Joseph assisted him (in many cases) to the point where he articulated, 'It's good for me to talk to you about this Ann' and 'if you have any other questions . . . I'm happy to answer them anytime,' indicating a further desire to chat. By providing an opportunity for him to speak (in this case to me) and pray (with his priest) he was assisted in his spiritual development.

Chris

My last patient interviewed was 'Chris' who, when we were introduced, seemed keen to talk to me. The RN alluded to my study on spirituality and he stated 'I need some of that.'

Chris began by addressing his reasons for admission. He had been very well until one year ago, when he began to feel unwell following an influenza vaccination. At 78 years of age he decided to return to his local doctor:

> Chris: I went to see the local doctor and he took a blood sample . . . (Well at 9 o'clock the next morning he said 'right you're into hospital because you've got a couple of weeks to live.' That's how rapid it was. A couple of weeks to live . . . They said 'you've got kidney failure.'

As he had been in the acute care setting previously, I asked him what prompted his admission to the hospice:

> Chris: Umm. I'm just trying to think when that occurred. It's not so very long ago. It's only a week or so ago. And I felt here is another opportunity . . . (. . .) And I'd heard that the . . . (. . .) hospice was very good, the treatment was excellent and the conditions were excellent and I thought that well, this is just something that I shouldn't ignore. . . .

Spirituality for Chris

Due to his previous comment that he 'needed some of that' I was interested to note how we could assist him. On interview, he was clear that his spirituality did not fit within the confines of any religion. As the conversation progressed, he did not allude to his former comment at all, seeming to deny a spiritual domain. Given this, I attempted to locate his frame of reference for spiritual issues:

Researcher: Since you've been here, what sort of things . . . do you have a religion in your life? . . . Do you think about an afterlife?

Chris: I've been asked that question more recently than ever before. But generally the answer is, the simple answer is 'no.' But that's not true. I feel it's not true. My religion is one of nature that the leaves on the trees get to the stage where they fall off and its a normal process there's no big deal about it.

Chris: As far as the afterlife is concerned, I don't believe that there is.

Researcher: So . . . is there a spiritual dimension? Does that feature anywhere?

Chris: It depends entirely on what you mean by a 'spiritual dimension.' Yes I think there is a spiritual dimension in so far as we all have a spirit, which is always the stronger or lessor or certainly affects your life. And all this talk of Buddhism and the Eastern religions and that sort of thing, it's all to do with spiritualism but behind it all I think there is a tremendous amount of what I call self hypnotism of hypnosis . . .

Researcher: Do you believe in a God? Is there a Supreme Being of any sort?

Chris: Yes, but I would call Him nature.

Chris's condition was serious, although his understanding of the hospice setting indicated that he did not view his placement here at this time as the end of his life. In the first few days of his hospitalisation, he maintained hope in the face of his illness. We talked of quality of life and I asked whether he looked into the future or was content to get through each day pain free:

Researcher: Is that the way you like to live your life one day at a time?

Chris: No. Not especially. I like to meet the current day in anticipation of what I expect it to be because I've a lot of expectations that haven't been realised yet. But in other words I'm never at a loss of what can I do now. So much to achieve. So much knowledge to acquire.

His final remarks indicated that he did not want to accept the finality of his life at this time:

Researcher: Was there anything else you'd like to say . . . ?

Chris: Only the obvious question . . . how long am I going to be here before I can get up and run around like a 2-year-old?

Summary and Discussion of Chris' Interview

Chris saw the hospice as 'another opportunity' and one he should not ignore. He obviously did not believe at that time that he had come there to die. Since his admission, he felt he had had 'excellent support' and following his remark that religion for him was aligned with nature, the nursing staff turned his bed to the leafy garden to allow him to spend the day looking outside (at this point he was unable to walk).

He believed 'there is a spiritual dimension in so far as we all have a spirit' but he aligned my question of a 'spiritual dimension' with 'Buddhism and the Eastern religions,' claiming it was all about 'spiritualism.'[1] His understanding of that concluded it was 'hypnosis.'

Chandler's Framework

Despite his initial comment that he 'needed some of that,' during our conversation Chris's remarks indicated he did not see much value in spiritual issues, as it is currently framed in an Eastern or Western belief. His religion (what might be called 'new' age), linked as it was with nature, meant natural things followed an ordered pattern and as such there was 'no big deal about it.'

The suddenness of his illness had caused him to only just begin to think about issues to do with spirituality. In Chandler's (1999) terms, Chris was beginning the journey. His responses regarding belief in an afterlife were interesting. 'I have been asked that question more recently than ever before' suggests that at least those around him had been thinking of this issue, which went some way to causing him to also consider spiritual issues. His 'the simple answer is no. But that's not true. I feel it's not true' may indicate that although he had begun his quest, at this point in his life, it was not clarified. Part of the lack of resolution may have been his desire to live more of his life, as there were many unful-filled expectations and dreams that he had not realised yet. He felt there was much more to accomplish at this stage in his life, 'So much to achieve. So much knowledge to acquire.'

In these beginning days of his spiritual quest, he was somewhat of a paradox. He believed in a spiritual dimension 'so far as we all have a spirit . . . or certainly affects your life,' yet, at this point he did not seem to be able to articulate what effect it might have. Moreover, his opening remark 'I need some of that,' indicated he was aware of some deficit in his own life, yet given the opportunity he did not elaborate on any need in this area. He was someone with whom I would have preferred to spend more time in an attempt to assist him uncover these beginning spiritual yearnings.

His concluding remark 'How long am I going to be here before I can get up and run around like a 2-year-old?' supports the fact that in Chandler's (1999) terms, the shock of his diagnosis meant he was still coming to terms with his impending death and understandably 'denial' featured quite largely in his thinking. He viewed the hospice setting as another opportunity to live, something that he should not ignore. At the same time he viewed 'spirituality' as 'spiritism,' aligning it with death. Therefore, at this point in his life, whilst seeking to live, he was not in-terested in addressing a topic that in his opinion related to death.

SUMMARY AND CONCLUSION

In drawing out aspects of patient's interviews, an attempt has been made to identify components of each person's spiritual journey. Under-taking this exercise serves to reinforce previous work, that to ade-quately care for the spiritual domain, there is a need for health care providers to get in touch with their own spirituality (Friedemann, Mouch & Racey 2002; McSherry & Draper 1998; Nolan & Crawford 1997; Harrington 1995; Shelly & Fish 1988).

It should be pointed out that conflict may arise if the health care pro-vider and the patient are at different ends of Chandler's continuum. If a patient was at stage three (ready to discuss spiritual issues) and the health care provider was at stage one (with a beginning awareness), spiritual issues may not be raised. Further, as health care providers (par-ticularly nurses) are 'brokers' to chaplaincy services, if spiritual issues are not a priority to the nurse, referral to these services may not occur. If, however, the patient is at stage one and the nurse at stage three, even if the patient is not prepared to discuss issues, those at stage three will at least be open to 'cues' if they present themselves. In other words, it is the *nurse* or *health care providers' spiritual development* that is the crucial factor.

It has been claimed that patients and relatives *are* open to a discussion regarding issues of spirituality (Swinton & Narayanasamy 2002; Bolmsjo 2000; Ross 1994) and the patients in this study reinforced that view. Notwithstanding that I only spoke to those who had agreed, here they were all keen to speak to someone. Even though one patient (Erica) classed spiritual issues as personal, she too agreed to speak to me. This study has shown that patients and relatives viewed this area as a topic for conversation and reaffirms that those working and living with the dying need to be 'in touch with their own spirit' (English 1998, p. 86). Being aware of spiritual journeys of patients, gives health care providers guidance to assist with spiritual care.

NOTE

1. Spiritualism (sometimes called 'spiritism') began around 1843 with a New York cobbler named Andrew Davis who claimed to be able to communicate with the spirits of the dead (Stevens 1995, p. 12). The emphasis of this thesis is (despite the lack of a definition) on spirituality and is not aligned to spiritism. Spirituality is a recognition that each person has a spirit and seeks to understand the state of development of that spirit. In other words, it is research into the living, not the dead.

REFERENCES

Balk, D. (1999). 'Bereavement and spiritual change.' *Death Studies,* 23 6, 485-493, September.

Blackburn, S. (1996). *Oxford Dictionary of Philosophy*. Oxford: Oxford University Press.

Bolmsjo, I. (2000). 'Existential issues in palliative care-Interviews with cancer patients.' *Journal of Palliative Care,* 16, 20-24.

Campbell, J. (1968). *The hero with a thousand faces*. Bollingen Series XVII, 2nd ed. Princeton, New Jersey: Princeton University Press.

Chandler, E. (1999). 'Spirituality.' *The Hospice Journal,* 14, 3/4, 63-74.

Derrickson, B.S. (1996). 'The spiritual work of the dying: A framework and case studies.' *The Hospice Journal,* 11, 2, 3-16.

Eisenberg, D.M., Davis, R.B., Eltner, S.L., Appel, S. Wilkey, S., Van Rompay, M. & Kesler, R.C. (1998). Trends in alternative medicine use in the United States, 1090-1997. *Journal of the American Medical Association* 280, 18, 1569-1575.

English, G. (1998). 'This is it! An approach to spirituality' in J. Parker & S. Aranda (Eds.), *Palliative Care: Explorations and Challenges*. Sydney: Maclennan & Petty.

Fleming, R. (2002). 'Depression and spirituality in Australian Aged Care Homes,' in E. MacKinlay (ed.) (2002). *Mental Health and Spirituality in Late Life*. New York: The Haworth Press Inc., 107-116.

Fowler, J. (1981). *Stages of faith. The psychology of human development and the quest for meaning*. Blackburn, Victoria: Dove Communications.

Friedemann, M.L., Mouch, J., & Racey, T. (2002). 'Nursing the spirit: The framework of systemic organization,' *Journal of Advanced Nursing* 39, 4, 325-332.

Harrington, A. (1995). 'Spiritual care: What does it mean to RNs?' *Australian Journal of Advanced Nursing*, 12, 4, 5-14, June-August.

Harrington, A. (1993). 'Registered Nurses Perceptions of Spiritual Care. A descriptive study.' Unpublished Masters thesis, Adelaide South Australia: The Flinders University.

Harris, S. M. (1998). 'Finding a forest among trees: Spirituality hiding in family therapy theories.' *Journal of Family Studies*, 4, 1, 77-86, April.

Irion, P. (1988). 'Treatment of the relationship of hospice to the church, interpreting the work for one another.' *Hospice and Ministry*.

Koenig, H.G., McCullough, M.E., & Larson, D.B. (2001). *Handbook of Religion and Health*. Oxford: Oxford University Press.

Koestenbaum, P. (1976). *Is there an answer to death?* Englewood Cliffs, New Jersey: Prentice-Hall.

Kuuppelomaki, M. (2001). 'Spiritual support for terminally ill patients: Nursing staff assessments.' *Journal of Clinical Nursing*, 10, 600-670.

McSherry, W., & Draper, P. (1998) 'The debates emerging from the literature surrounding the concept of spirituality as applied to nursing.' *Journal of Advanced Nursing* 27, 4, 683-691.

Millison, M., & Dudley, J.R. (1992). 'Providing spiritual support: A job for all hospice professionals.' *The Hospice Journal*, 8, 4, 49-66.

Moberg, D.O. (2001). 'Research on spirituality' in D.O. Moberg (ed). *Ageing and spirituality. Spiritual dimensions of aging theory, research, practice and policy*. New York: The Haworth Press, Inc. 55-69.

Moore, T. (1992). *Care of the soul. A guide for cultivating depth and sacredness in everyday life*. New York: Harper Collins.

Nolan, P., & Crawford, P. (1997). 'Towards a rhetoric of spirituality in mental health care.' *Journal of Advanced Nursing*, 26, 2, 289-294.

Peck, S.M. (1987). *The different drum*. London: Arrow Books.

Perlman, D., & Takacs, G.J. (1990). 'The 10 stages of change.' *Nursing Management*, 21, 4, 33-38, April.

Pryor, R.J. (1989). *Some reading for the journey. An annotated bibliography on spiritual formation in theological education*. Kew, Victoria: The Commission on Continuing Education for Ministry.

Redding, S. (2000). 'Control theory in dying: What do we know?' *American Journal of Hospice and Palliative Care*, 17, 3, 204-208, May/June.

Ross, L. (1994). 'The spiritual dimension: Its importance to patients' health, well-being, and quality of life and its implications for nursing practice.' *International Journal of Nursing Studies*, 32, 5, 457-468.

Shelly, J.A., & Fish, S. (1988) *Spiritual care the nurse's role* (3rd ed.). Illinois: Inter-Varsity Press.

Swinton, J., & Narayanasamy, A. (2002). 'Response to: "A critical view of spirituality and spiritual assessment."' *Journal of Advanced Nursing*, 40, 2, 158.

The Holy Bible (1984). New International Version. Grand Rapids Michigan: Zondervan Publishing House.

Thoresen, C. (1999.) 'Spirituality and health: Is there a relationship?' *Journal of Health Psychology*, 4, 3, 291-300.

Non-Speech Based Pastoral Care:
A Pastoral Care Program for Aged Care Residents with Little or No Ability to Speak

Elizabeth Vreugdenhil, PhD

SUMMARY. Pastoral care depends on the ability to communicate, most commonly through the medium of speech. The aged person who has suffered illness or accident that has adversely affected their speech, is in great need of pastoral care. Yet chaplains and pastoral carers can feel helpless in the face of such a significant deficit and may not know what to do. At Tregenza Avenue Aged Care Service, the Chaplaincy service has developed helpful individual programs for non-speech based pastoral care. Using visual and tactile symbols, pictures, touch, and music, we have been able to minister to people with a variety of speech problems, with promising results. *[Article copies available for a fee from The Haworth Document Delivery Service: 1-800-HAWORTH. E-mail address: <docdelivery@haworthpress.com> Website: <http://www.HaworthPress.com> © 2004 by The Haworth Press, Inc. All rights reserved.]*

Rev. Dr. Elizabeth Vreugdenhil is affiliated with Tregenza Avenue Aged Care Service, Metropolitan Domiciliary Care, South Australia, 8 David Avenue, Black Forest, South Australia, 5035, Australia (E-mail: elger@adam.com.au).

The author gratefully acknowledges the invaluable assistance of Speech Pathologist Stacey Attrill, and the work and dedication of Pastoral Visitors Rosemarie Buss and Eda Klement, and Diversional Therapist Donna Bainbridge.

[Haworth co-indexing entry note]: "Non-Speech Based Pastoral Care: A Pastoral Care Program for Aged Care Residents with Little or No Ability to Speak." Vreugdenhil, Elizabeth. Co-published simultaneously in *Journal of Religious Gerontology* (The Haworth Pastoral Press, an imprint of The Haworth Press, Inc.) Vol. 16, No. 3/4, 2004, pp. 147-160; and: *Spirituality of Later Life: On Humor and Despair* (ed: Rev. Elizabeth MacKinlay) The Haworth Pastoral Press, an imprint of The Haworth Press, Inc., 2004, pp. 147-160. Single or multiple copies of this article are available for a fee from The Haworth Document Delivery Service [1-800-HAWORTH, 9:00 a.m. - 5:00 p.m. (EST). E-mail address: docdelivery@haworthpress.com].

KEYWORDS. Pastoral care, speech, aphasia, dysarthria, life's meaning, aged, dementia

INTRODUCTION

Elderly people living in residential care, who have lost their speech or who have only limited speech, are often marginalised. Cohen and Eisdorfer (1986) write, "When patients lose verbal competence, families tend to talk about the patient less as a person and more as an object; even when the patient is sitting in the same room" (Cohen and Eisdorfer 1986:153). Residents of aged care facilities often experience this from both families and staff. People do not mean to be unkind but someone who cannot speak properly is unconsciously perceived as being less than an adult human being. Aged care residents suffer greatly when they lose their speech in addition to losing other abilities.

A resident suffering from dementia and complete loss of speech used an alphabet board to communicate. One day as the Pastoral Visitor sat with her, she spelled out the words, "die, die, die."

A nursing home resident wheeled herself up to the chaplain in a wheelchair. She was suffering from dementia and was losing the ability to speak. The chaplain introduced herself stating her name and role. "Hello, I'm Elizabeth, the chaplain." The resident replied, "I'm dead, I'm dead. There is no God, there is no God." She paused and then said in a puzzled tone. "I love God."

The distress of these two women was plain to see. They both knew that their disability was profound and each felt that she might as well be dead. Her disability created a deep spiritual dilemma for the second woman. How could a loving God, whom she also loved, do such a thing to her?

People without adequate speech are in great need of spiritual and pastoral care, yet they are very difficult to help. Conventional pastoral care depends to a large extent on conversation. Hersh (1998) writes,

> Conversation is fundamental to virtually all aspects of our lives. Conversation . . . does not just entail information exchange, sharing opinions or feelings, demanding and requesting. It is also the way the individuals assert themselves socially and form relationships with others. . . . (Our) most basic way of initiating, maintaining and enriching our social life is through conversation, and it is

through conversation that we gain a sense of well-being and self-worth. (Hersh 1998:2)

Conversation is an essential part of pastoral care. Listening attentively and empathically to the stories of the person being helped is a most important pastoral skill. Discussion of some aspect of a person's situation so that they can come to greater understanding, is also essential. If the client cannot speak, or understand speech very well, it is difficult to give satisfactory pastoral care. This was the problem that faced the pastoral care team at Tregenza Avenue Aged Care Service (TAACS). Residents without speech were being neglected pastorally and spiritually and a way needed to be found to reach them.

Tregenza Avenue Aged Care Service (TAACS)

TAACS is a state government residential aged care facility in Elizabeth, South Australia. It consists of seventy high care and low care beds (nursing home and hostel). There is also a community centre and a comprehensive diversional therapy program. The chaplaincy service comprises the ecumenical coordinating chaplain, who is employed, and eight voluntary pastoral visitors who are recruited from local churches. There is also a visiting Catholic chaplain and pastoral visitor.

Most of the programs at TAACS related to the social, cultural, pastoral and spiritual care of the residents depend on the resident possessing an adequate degree of speech. It is much more difficult to care for the residents who cannot speak and this means that they are often kept on the margins, watching what is going on rather than actively participating. Yet in the Christian faith, the marginalised ones are the ones who are to be most highly regarded. The pastoral care team felt that it was imperative to try to reach and care for the marginalised people who could not speak.

Understanding the Disability

The first step in helping those without speech was to understand the nature of their disability so that methods for communicating with them could be found. With the help of the Speech Pathologist we learned that there are two main types of speech disability: aphasia and dysarthria.

Aphasia is defined as "a breakdown of language skills affecting speaking, understanding, reading and writing, which occurs after brain damage, most commonly following a stroke" (Hersh 1998:Appendix H). If a person suffers a stroke the damage may result immediately in aphasia; however, their memory and intelligence may be unimpaired. If a person suffers dementia then the onset of aphasia is gradual. There will also be memory loss and evidence of poor judgement. Sometimes a person who suffers from a stroke also develops dementia.

Although some people cannot produce words easily, they can understand everything that is said to them. Others however also suffer from receptive aphasia. The sufferer may feel that they are in a foreign country where the language is unknown. They cannot understand anything that is said to them (Nichols 2003). They may also have problems writing as there "may be difficulty remembering how to form letters, spell words or organise thoughts and ideas in a way that can be expressed on paper" (Hersh 1998:Appendix I).

Dysarthria is defined as ". . . a speech disorder that is due to a weakness or incoordination of the speech muscles. Speech is slow, weak, imprecise or uncoordinated. . . . In adults, dysarthria can be caused by stroke, degenerative disease (Parkinson's, Huntington's), . . . infections (meningitis, brain tumours) and toxins (drug or alcohol abuse) . . ." (Styba 2003). Sometimes the dysarthria is so severe that the person cannot be understood at all and needs to use an alphabet board. However, people suffering from dysarthria know which words they wish to use and they can understand speech.

It is important to know the correct diagnosis when a person suffers speech difficulties so that an appropriate method of communication is used. When someone cannot speak properly it is often assumed that they cannot understand, but this may not be the case.

An aged care resident was unable to make herself understood at all and could only produce unintelligible sounds. It was assumed that because she could not communicate, her understanding must also be impaired. She became easily frustrated and physically attacked the staff by scratching and pinching. She often screamed loudly. After a speech pathology assessment it was discovered that she was suffering from severe dysarthria. She could understand everything that was said to her and was given an alphabet board to help her communicate by spelling out the words she wished to say. Her aggressive behaviour decreased markedly when people communicated with her in a more appropriate way and she could make herself understood.

Another important consideration when communicating with aged people is possible hearing and/or sight impairment. Many elderly people suffer from both these disabilities. They may need hearing aids to hear and glasses to see so that they can lip read. Sometimes, when staff are very busy they may forget to put in the hearing aids and put on the glasses. Without speech the person cannot ask for what they need. The pastoral carer needs to be alert to this and ask for the resident's glasses and hearing aids to be used.

Sight impairment may also occur from a stroke if the optic nerve is involved, so it is important to be aware of the resident's range of vision.

A resident had suffered a serious stroke on the left side of her brain. In addition to complete loss of speech, she was unable to see anything on her right side. She also had a narrow range of vision on her left, and could only see from her nose to about the middle of her left eye. Her pastoral visitor needed to position herself so that she was in the resident's field of vision. Sitting too far to either side meant that she was unable to be seen.

The Spiritual and Emotional Cost of Losing Speech

Most people enjoy talking with family and friends when feelings and stories can be shared. However, if the ability to do this is lost through an inability to speak, then the sense of intimacy with the other is damaged, the relationship suffers and may break down. The person who cannot speak feels isolated and lacking in friendship and companionship. This is very serious as relationships give meaning to our lives. Elizabeth MacKinlay (2001) writes that "Meaning expressed through human relationship involves support and the need for connection with others" (MacKinlay 2001:203). According to MacKinlay, in old age we seek to make sense of life and have spiritual tasks peculiar to that stage of our lives. We look for the ultimate meaning in life that may be expressed as a belief in God. In response to this ultimate meaning, an important spiritual task is to develop and maintain intimate, meaningful relationships with others (MacKinlay 2001:42). As a lack of speech can seriously impair the ability to relate to others, with a subsequent loss of intimacy, the person without speech may experience a loss of meaning in life. This leads them towards a sense of despair and can cause the sufferer to lose their sense of God and God's love. Hence the woman referred to above, who said bitterly, "There is no God, there is no God."

Building an empathic, warm and non-judgemental pastoral relationship with a person who has experienced loss of speech, can be a means of giving their life some meaning and bringing to them a sense of a loving God. Even if a person suffering from dementia may not be able to remember the pastoral carer from one visit to the next, the relationship is still valuable. The sense of well-being that is engendered from a warm, loving encounter will last throughout the day, even though the memory of the actual event may disappear.

Building a Relationship

In consultation with the speech pathologist the pastoral care team decided to try to build pastoral relationships with several high care residents who had speech difficulties. The pastoral care program in relation to three of these residents is discussed below. The pastoral visitors used visual symbols, touch and music in addition to speech. The visual symbols consisted of small wooden crosses, pictures, and bible story picture books. Recorded music consisted of well-known hymns of God's love and music known to be enjoyed by the resident. Touch involved holding the resident's hand or giving them a hug if this was appropriate. Simple puzzles were also used for recreation and fun. Even though the medium for the establishment of the relationship was childlike at times, the attitude of the team members towards the residents was that of one adult relating to another (Bell 1997:117).

Hints for Good Communication-Sending the Message

Communication is a two way process which involves both sending messages and receiving them. When communicating with a person who cannot speak, we need to do all that we can to send the right message to the person, that is, they are a valued human being. Following are some hints that may help the pastoral carer to do this.

The pastoral carer tries to choose a quiet place for the pastoral encounter, which usually lasts about 30 minutes. People who have suffered brain damage of any kind find it difficult to concentrate if there are too many stimuli bombarding them at once. It is important to turn off the radio and television, and if possible, talk to the resident on their own (Mace 1991:39). Make sure you are at eye level with the person so that they can see your face. If there is a hearing deficit then the person may need to read your lips.

First impressions are important so always call the person by name so that they know you are talking to them (Bell, 1997:116). Introduce yourself by name and role; for example, "Hello Mrs Smith, my name is Elizabeth and I am the chaplain." If a person suffers from dementia it may be necessary to do this every time you meet because they may be unable to remember you.

When talking to someone who has limited or no speech, use a calm, low-pitched voice and take your time. Watch your tone of voice as it is very easy to talk down to someone with a speech impairment. It is most important to establish a relationship between equals. Use short words and short simple sentences and give the person plenty of time to respond. Ask one question at a time, recognising however that some people may not be able to cope with yes and no responses, and may shake or nod their head indiscriminately. Remember that the person will have difficulty in processing the words that you say and will not understand rapid speech (Bell 1997:39).

Communication-Receiving the Message

As well as doing everything possible to communicate with the aged person it is also necessary to try to understand what is being said. This process is helped if there is some knowledge of the person's life history and their interests. If the person has little of no speech then it is necessary to learn to read their body language. Speech is really only a small part of communication but we tend to concentrate on this as though it is all that matters. However, attending to body language can tell us much about the messages that a person wishes to communicate.

Richard Fleming (1999) has developed an excellent resource to help families and carers of residents suffering from dementia, who have limited communication. The resource is known as the "Emotional Responses in Care" (ERIC) assessment tool. The goal of ERIC is to help "the ordinary person recognise and record a manageable number of key signs, that indicate areas of satisfaction and dissatisfaction" (Fleming 1999:2). The carer is encouraged to observe the resident each day and record on a chart the emotions that the resident displays in response to particular activities. The emotions are as in Table 1.

The pastoral visitors found it easier to keep a diary of the emotions of the resident rather than use the scoring method provided. Keeping the diary helped the pastoral visitors to identify the particular way that each resident expressed themselves. It also helped them to attend carefully to the non-verbal communication.

THREE CASE STUDIES

Following are three case studies that demonstrate the above principles in practice.

TABLE 1. Emotional Responses in Care

Name of emotional state	Descriptors (signs to look for)	Comments
Pleasure	The person smiles, laughs, has crinkled "smiling" eyes, nods in pleasant agreement, reaches out in welcome.	An active emotion, it involves responding to a situation.
Warmth and affection	The person gives emotional support to others or responds affectionately when approached.	Sometimes it involves a touch or a cuddle.
Helpfulness (Spontaneous)	The person attempts to help other people without being asked.	"Attempts" does not necessarily mean he or she is successful at the task that is being attempted.
Anger	The person clenches teeth, grimaces, shouts, curses, pushes, threatens to be or is aggressive.	Usually easily recognised.
Anxiety/Fear	The person has a furrowed brow, is restless, makes repeated or agitated movements, sighs, withdraws from a person or a situation, trembles, has tight facial muscles, calls repetitively, wrings hands, jiggles legs, has wide open eyes.	The calling or shouting sounds quite different from that found in anger.
Physical discomfort or pain	The person rubs or holds a spot on their body, limps, moans or screws up their face.	Not an emotion but certainly affects the way people feel.
Helpfulness (prompted)	The person attempts to help other people when asked.	Asked means asked once or twice, not bargained with or bullied.
Sadness	The person cries, has tears, moans, has a turned down mouth, has eyes/head down turned and an expressionless face, keeps wiping eyes.	
Creativity and expressiveness (Spontaneous)	The person involves themselves in activities such as dancing, singing, artwork, etc., when they are available without being asked.	Quality of output (song, dance, painting or pattern of peas on a plate) is totally irrelevant.
Contentment	The person sits or lies in a comfortable, relaxed way. There is no tension in their limbs or neck. Movements are slow and relaxed.	A passive, relaxed form of pleasure.

Case Study One-Isa

Isa was in her mid-nineties when she died. She had suffered a number of strokes and also suffered from Parkinson's disease. When the pastoral visitor began seeing her Isa had lost her speech, and could not walk, stand or sit. She could only move her left arm and her left knee. She had difficulty in moving the muscles in her face and so most of the time her face was expressionless except for her eyes. During the pastoral sessions Isa would gaze intently and intelligently at the pastoral visitor. Isa spent her days in a large bed chair in the nursing home lounge room.

Most of the time she was immobile and on the surface, did not appear to be taking anything in. However, it became apparent that she was aware of what was going on around her.

Isa was a devoutly religious woman who had been a church organist for 40 years. She had learned to play several other musical instruments and had accompanied her husband when he sang at concerts and in church. She had belonged to various choirs and had loved singing herself. Isa attended the nursing home church services but it was felt that she would also benefit from individual pastoral care. The pastoral visitor saw Isa each week for a 30 minute session. She would take Isa's hand, greet her and identify herself. Isa would turn her eyes towards her and watch her intently for the duration of the session. The pastoral visitor would read a short simple bible passage, very slowly and with many pauses. On one occasion the pastoral visitor felt that the passage she had chosen was too long so she stopped halfway through and said, "We'll read the rest next week." Immediately, Isa placed her hand firmly on the bible so that it could not be shut. The pastoral visitor got the message and continued reading. On another occasion, she forgot her bible and apologised to Isa, saying that they could have the reading next week. Isa turned her eyes away from the pastoral visitor and would not look at her. It was only after several more apologies that Isa would look at her again. Despite many handicaps Isa managed to communicate strongly with eye movements and one hand.

After the bible reading, they sometimes listened to music. The first time the pastoral visitor showed Isa a small wooden cross, Isa grasped it very firmly and would not let it go. It was a tactile prayer. The pastoral visitor often showed picture postcards to Isa and would talk about them. It was discovered later that Isa had loved to travel so this activity was appreciated. The postcards were followed by a puzzle as people who cannot speak need to be able to enjoy themselves. It is important that the activities and puzzles are failure free activities as disabled residents daily experience their inability to perform even simple tasks and this is detrimental to their self-esteem. Successfully completing a simple game boosts their sense of self worth (Sheridan 1987:5). Isa loved the monkey-puzzle, which consists of a number of pictures that need to be matched. It is impossible to fail as all the halves match even if the colours are different. Isa would concentrate hard on the monkey puzzle game, holding out her hand for another piece when she was ready. At the end of the session, the pastoral visitor would take Isa's hand, say a short prayer, and then say goodbye and wave. It is important to wave so that the person knows that you are going and they are staying. Isa would continue to watch her until she was out of sight.

In the last few weeks of her life, Isa continued to respond with arm and knee movements and her eyes. On one occasion she was sitting staring blankly into space until a CD of a violin concerto was played for her. Immediately she began to move her arm and her leg. It was not possible to precisely name the particular emotions that Isa was experiencing but it was obvious that the music moved her strongly. The arm and knee movements were the only way she could indicate her response to the music.

Case Study Two-Joan

Joan is an 88 year old woman suffering from dementia. She can no longer walk and has developed aphasia. She has great difficulty in finding words, but occasionally she is surprisingly fluent. Joan has found her loss of speech very difficult to cope with. She becomes depressed at times and is angry about her condition. Joan sometimes becomes very upset at night but was observed singing "Jesus loves me" to herself, which helped her sleep.

Until she came to TAACS, Joan had not attended church since her childhood. However like many residents Joan searched for meaning in her suffering and found the church services helpful. When her speech began to fail significantly, it was felt that she would benefit from individual pastoral care. The pastoral visitor talked to Joan about this and Joan agreed to participate. Sometimes Joan smiles, accepts her and participates in the program. At other times she becomes angry and waves the pastoral visitor away, saying, "No God today."

When Joan is in the mood, she listens with the pastoral visitor to well known hymns on tape and then they sing them together. Joan is very musical and was part of a singing group before she became ill. The part of the brain which "stores" music has not been damaged and so Joan still enjoys singing. It often happens that a person can enjoy music and sing songs even though their ability to speak is impaired (Bell 1997:135).

Joan enjoys looking through a children's bible story book which has many pictures of the Jesus stories. On one occasion she recognised a picture of Mary holding the baby Jesus and was able to fluently and confidently recount the story. She enjoyed the experience which gave her a sense of mastery as words usually present such a problem for her. Joan also enjoys looking at pictures while the pastoral visitor talks about them. She says a few words when she is able. Joan's communication is quite clear from her facial expressions, body language and the few words she can speak.

On one occasion Joan showed concern for the pastoral visitor. The visitor was pushing Joan in her wheelchair as they were going out for a walk. As she struggled with the heavy door, Joan said "Mind out love, Don't hurt yourself." The pastoral visitor was touched at Joan's concern for her welfare, especially after enduring so much rejection.

Joan is very frustrated with her lack of speech. The continued presence of the pastoral visitor each week, even if Joan rejects her occasionally, represents God's continuing love and care for her during an exceptionally difficult time of her life.

Case Study Three-Rose

Rose is an eighty-seven-year-old widow who suffered a very severe stroke on the left side of her brain. She has global aphasia, which means that she cannot speak or understand speech. However it is thought that she may be able to understand a little. Rose does not have dementia and is able to remember who people are. She cannot walk, stand or sit and can only move her left hand. Her face is very expressive. Her vision is limited as the optic nerve was damaged during the stroke. She cannot see at all on the right side of her body and has a narrow range of vision in her left eye. It is important for the pastoral visitor to understand this as sitting on Rose's right side, or too far to her left means that Rose is unaware of her presence.

Unlike the previous two people, Rose's condition happened suddenly and was not the result of a slow deterioration. The stroke shocked her family and friends and most likely herself. She becomes depressed and sad at times as no doubt, she grieves for all that she has lost. However, at other times she appears to be contented and is kind and gentle towards the staff. She has a beautiful smile and graciously extends her hand in greeting to anyone who speaks to her. If she wants something to stop she indicates this with her hand.

Rose has been a member of her church throughout her life. She is brought to all the church services at TAACS and is regularly visited by her pastor, family and friends. It was felt that she would benefit from the pastoral care program.

The pastoral visitor sees Rose each week for thirty minutes. Rose becomes tired if the session is longer than that. At the beginning of the session the pastoral visitor approaches Rose and introduces herself. She is graciously received with a smile and a squeeze of her hand. As Rose has read the bible all her life the pastoral visitor holds up the bible for Rose to see so that she knows what is being read to her. Then, sitting beside Rose, she reads a few verses about God's love, very slowly, pointing to the words as she says them. Rose looks at the bible with her. Even though Rose may not understand many of the words, she responds positively to this experience of pastoral care. After the bible reading, the pastoral visitor may show Rose some pictures or postcards and talk about them. This is followed by some puzzles, which may be a posting box or the monkey-puzzle. Rose studies the puzzle with great concentration and shows pleasure in her face when the puzzle is completed. This is an important part of the process as many people without speech are not given anything to do that is intellectually challenging. Finally the pastoral visitor holds Rose's hand and says a short prayer with her. Then she says goodbye and Rose waves to her.

Rose does not always complete the full program. Sometimes she is very down cast and just shakes her head, so the pastoral visitor just sits with her for a while and holds her hand. On other occasions she will listen intently to the bible reading but is not interested in anything else and waves the pictures and puzzles away. However, she is usually willing to try and indicates her enjoyment with her smiles, her hand movements and her intense concentration. The presence of the pastoral visitor enables her to experience God's love, and gives her an opportunity to pray and to experience the bible being read. It also provides a sense of intimacy with a friend, which is so important in finding and maintaining a sense of meaning in old age.

Caring for the Carers

This is very difficult work for the volunteer pastoral visitors as the residents do not improve and will eventually die in the Nursing Home. It is painful to watch someone with whom you have developed a relationship, slowly and inevitably deteriorate. At TAACS the staff and volunteers have as their aim, that every resident should live as fully as possible until they die. Even if today is worse than yesterday, it is still important that today is the best that it could be. However, it is emotionally demanding work and the pastoral visitors need to be supported through this experience.

Further Developments

This work is in its initial stages at TAACS and there is much to be done. Training sessions have been held with other staff. As a result of this the diversional therapist and the care staff have incorporated the ideas into their practice and have further developed them. The affect and level of activity of the resident is recorded before each intervention, and compared with the affect and level of activity during the intervention and afterwards. The initial results are promising and have encouraged the staff to persevere with these residents.

CONCLUSION

People with limited or no speech are often isolated and therefore emotionally and spiritually abandoned by others. This has a detrimental effect on their sense of self-esteem and meaning in life. It can lead to a feeling of having been abandoned by God. The abandonment by others occurs because pastoral carers and others do not know how to cope with people with severe speech impairment even though there is a strong desire to help. The non-speech based pastoral care program, developed at TAACS gives these residents appropriate spiritual and pastoral support. It has been demonstrated that visual symbols, music and touch are used with good effect to communicate with the residents who cannot speak. Their non-verbal communication is carefully observed and used in the communication exchange.

Each of the residents described above formed a good relationship with their pastoral visitor. Even though their speech was limited or non-existent, an experience of intimacy was made possible and therefore a sense of meaning and hope was engendered.

REFERENCES

Bell, V., & Troxel, D. (1997). *The Best Friends Approach to Alzheimer's Care.* London: MacLennan and Petty.

Cohen, D., & Eisdorfer, C. (1986). *The Loss of Self: A Family Resource for the Care of Alzheimer's Disease and related Disorders.* Ontario: Plume.

Fleming, R. (1999). Dementia Services Development Centre. *Beyond Words: Emotional Responses as Quality Indicators in Dementia Care.* Australia, Commonwealth Department of Health and Aged Care.

Hersh, D. (1998). *Making Conversation: A Handbook for Running Talkback Groups for Chronic Aphasia.* Woodville, South Australia: Queen Elizabeth Hospital Research Foundation.

Mace, N., & Rabins, P.V. (1991). *The 36-Hour Day (revised edition).* Baltimore: The Johns Hopkins University Press.

MacKinlay, E. (2001). *The Spiritual Dimension of Ageing*. London and Philadelphia: Jessica Kingsley Publishers.

Nichols, T. (2003). *Bungalow Software for rehabilitation from stroke, aphasia, and head injuries*. Available from World Wide Web: *http://www.strokesupport.com/info/aphasia/what_aphasia_is.htm*.

Sheridan, C. (1987). *Failure-Free Activities for the Alzheimer's Patient*. San Francisco: Cottage Books.

Styba, L. (2003). *The Speech-Language Pathology Website*. Available from World Wide Web: *http://home.ica.net/~fred/anch10-1.htm*.

Index

Made in the USA
Lexington, KY
20 April 2016